A Walk on the Beach

by Sandy Klingspon

Trinity Products, LLC.

A Walk on the Beach by Sandy Klingspon

Copyright © 2017

Published by Trinity Products, LLC.

Edited by Sony Elise. www.sonyelise.com

ISBN 978099356104

Printed in the United States of America

January

"Walk on the beach...you are worth it."

Steady Waves

It was one of those days. The problems I had been dealing with got to me. I was so ready to figure things out and be done with it. I ran to my escape—Weko Beach. It's where I meet up with God. There I could clear my head and figure out what I needed to do.

We've all been there, facing something we'd rather not be facing. We try to think and reason things out. We do what we know to do, and the problems still don't go away. We may even pray and talk with God about it like I did that day on Weko Beach. Nothing.

I didn't hear answers to my prayers or ways to solve any of my problems. All I heard was the steady pounding of waves. Psalm 29:3 says that the voice of the Lord is on the waters. It was the steady pounding of the waves that comforted me and made me forget for a bit why I was there.

Listen … the steady waves may be God speaking.

"The voice of the Lord is over the waters."
- Psalm 29:3

Pick It Up

An Indian bead sat there along Lake Michigan. I was too lazy to pick it up, thinking it was big enough for me to see on my way back. Now I realized I wasn't going to find it. I should have picked it up when I had the chance.

Haven't we all foolishly let go of or lost something valuable? Maybe we were too lazy to do what it took to have or to hang onto it. Maybe we let it go because we felt guilty—we didn't deserve something so nice.

There is a purpose for everything under the sun. There is a purpose for hard times, but there is also a purpose for good times. You can learn from hard situations as well as good situations. Both come with valuable lessons. Just pick up and grab hold of them when you have the chance.

Don't let blessings pass by without grabbing them.

"There is a time for everything, and a season for every activity under the heavens."
- Ecclesiastes 3:1

Stinging Sand

The wind-blown grains of sand stung as they hit my legs. I couldn't enjoy my walk with sand blowing all over the place. Not really a day to be at the beach.

We all have days when we don't want to be out there participating in life. We'd rather be in our safe little corner of the world instead of getting hit by all that's blowing around. Things hurt. People mistreat us. Others leave us, whether by choice or by death. It stings. But there is hope.

Jesus came and died. Knowing and believing this gives you hope. Because He won the victory, all the hurts you face will one day be completely healed. You will be new without carrying any baggage around. You may not enjoy what is hitting you right now, but that's okay. Jesus won and ... the sting will go away.

"The sting of death is sin, and the power of sin is the law. But thanks be to God! He gives us the victory through our Lord Jesus Christ."
- 1 Corinthians 15:56-57

Different Stones

The stones along the beach come in all different sizes and shapes. There are big stones and tiny stones. Some are jagged while others are smooth. There are colorful ones with pizzazz and dull drab ones. Some even look like pieces of old concrete with small pebbles stuck to it.

What each of us can do comes in different sizes and shapes, like the stones on a beach. Some of us have a lot of talent in one area while the rest of us have a smaller amount of talent in that same area. Some of us come across a little rough around the edges while others easily connect with people. Still others of us seem boring while those around us shine with a bit more pizzazz.

God gives you talents to use for what He has planned for your life. Embrace your differences. Those are the abilities and attributes you need to do what God has you here to do.

Differences are an advantage.

"To one He gave five bags of gold, to another two bags, and to another one bag, each according to his ability."
- Matthew 25:15

Crying Sea Gulls

Sea gulls are not very timid birds. They cry out and surround people for whatever morsels of food they can get. I learned to put my food away when I'm done and to not leave it unattended on a beach blanket.

Have you ever worried about how to pay the next bill or where your next meal would come from? Life has a way of making us worry … making us wonder how we will get through things.

The sea gulls had the right idea. They cried out for food. Their cries can be loud and obnoxious, but we learn from their example. The Bible tells us to make our requests known to God. Cry out to Him. Don't be timid. Talk to Him about your worries and commit them to His care because He loves you, and He is the only one who knows best how to handle them. When you're done boldly crying out to God, pack up your worries and put them away. Let God carry them.

"Do not be anxious about anything but present your requests to God."
- Philippians 4:6

Beginning and Ending

I stood at the bottom of the steps and looked across the boardwalk. I could see my destination: the other side.

Every calling in life has a beginning and an ending. We put all our effort into something and it ends. It doesn't matter how honorable the calling is, it doesn't last. That can be discouraging, but it doesn't have to be.

When you think about it, Jesus had the most honorable calling in this life: to save and reconcile us to God. His life came to an end, but ... in the end salvation was found and new eternal beginnings became a reality.

Your endings are just as exciting as your beginnings when following Jesus. Callings begin and end in Him.

Follow Him.

"I am the Alpha and the Omega, the First and the Last, the Beginning and the End."
- Revelations 22:13

Beach Worthy

The day was beautiful. Summer was in full swing in Michigan. I could feel the warmth of the sun and see the blue sky. I walked along the beach wondering what it was that brought these people here today and what was keeping others away.

Life offers many opportunities for us to draw close to Jesus … yet we don't. Why? Maybe we feel ashamed or unworthy. We are like wanna-be beachgoers hiding inside on a beautiful summer day when we should be at the beach.

If you aren't spending time with God because you don't feel worthy, consider this: Jesus saw your worth so He died on the cross for you. Since He loves you enough to die for you, can you consider yourself worthy enough to spend time with Him? Now it's time to see your worth through the eyes of Jesus.

Take a walk along the Beach. You are worth it.

"Lord, don't trouble Yourself, for I do not deserve
to have You come under my roof."
- Luke 7:6

Should I?

Another day at the beach. Should I sit and watch the seagulls? Should I tan? Should I walk along the water's edge? As a child, I usually chose to swim. As a teenager, I chose to tan. As an adult, I choose to walk.

We have many choices during the course of a lifetime. The choices we make are affected by many things. Maybe it's age, maybe it's what we are into at the time, or maybe it's personal reasons. A common element affecting all our choices should be wisdom.

Numbering our days alludes to wisdom. It's making the most of what we have—whether in time, in knowledge, in foresight, in experience—to have a positive outcome. Whatever choices you end up making, it should lead you to a better, positive place than where you started. When you wisely number your days, it shows in the positive outcomes your decisions bring about.

Life is what you make it day-by-day. Start numbering.

"So teach us to number our days, that we may gain a heart of wisdom."
- Psalm 90:12

Lost Cause

I sat on the blanket watching the kids in the water as I blew up the plastic beach ball. They played with it for a bit and then forgot about it, leaving it to drift out on the lake. By the time we realized it, the ball was too far gone. We had to let it go. It was a lost cause.

You may face circumstances that seem like a lost cause … like there's nothing left to do but let it go. But God has a heart for restoring things. He sent Jesus to reconcile and restore our relationship to Himself. He can restore situations you thought were lost. He restores broken relationships and lost dreams.

We got our beach ball back. Someone farther down the beach saw it and brought it back to us.

God restores our lost causes.

"But I will restore you to health and heal your wounds." - Jeremiah 30:17

Deformed Beads

I picked it up even though it wasn't perfect. A chunk was missing. It was really only half an Indian bead but I would add it to my collection anyway.

We look at other people's lives and wonder why our lives aren't as good as theirs. Why did we have to go through this and they didn't? Did we do something wrong? Jesus' disciples wondered the same thing. They ran into a man blind since birth and asked Jesus why. Who sinned to cause his blindness?

Jesus' explained to His disciples that it happened to show the glory of God and then He healed the blind man. Jesus' response is the same today for you. He blesses you with people and circumstances you may sometimes forget are blessings because they aren't perfect. They are chipped, broken, or deformed like the bead I found. But you are given "deformed" blessings so God can be glorified.

Will you pick up your "deformed" blessings?

"Rabbi, who sinned, this man or his parents, that he was born blind?"
- John 9:2

Pressured

As I walked along Weko Beach, the wet sand became lighter when my foot pressed down into it. My weight pressured the water out with each step.

Deadlines, demands, and expectations that we place on ourselves, or that others place on us, seem to come out at every turn. It can re-arrange our day at the drop of a hat. Before we know it, the day is spent and our best intentions have fallen to the wayside. We miss our mark and the goals we had set.

When the unexpected happens and demands come pressuring you to spend time on them, what do you do? Your relationship with Jesus is important. If you are not careful, you will find life's demands pushing Him out much like my weight pressuring the water out of the sand.

Something that has worked for me: Spend time with Him first thing each day before the pressures start. What works for you?

"But the worries of this life, the deceitfulness of wealth and the desires for other things come in and choke the word, making it unfruitful."
– Mark 4:19

Not So Ho-Hum

The stones near the edge of the beach glistened after being swept over by the water. They almost looked shiny, not like the ones in the dry sand. As a kid picking up stones along Lake Michigan, I would always go for the shiny, colorful ones. They were my favorites but when they dried out, they didn't look so shiny. Another ho-hum stone.

We take pride in our abilities. We like to stand out for what we can do well and the things we can't do so well, we want to do better. It's like the stones. We want our abilities to shine. We don't want to be just another ho-hum average person.

Stones shine when washed over by the water. What you are able to do—your abilities—will stand out more. They will shine more when they are done with the help of the Lord. He is the One empowering you. He can take your abilities and turn them from ho-hum to shine.

Wash the ho-hum away and shine.

"The Lord make His face shine upon you and be gracious to you." - Numbers 6:25

Smells Fishy

The smell of dead fish was unmistakable. Not often do I walk along Weko Beach smelling dead fish, but when I do – I know I will run into them somewhere along the way.

We all run across situations in our lives when we know something isn't quite right. We sense it. Yet we continue on, hoping our senses are wrong. It's like walking on a beach with stinky dead fish and hoping not to run into any.

Part of growing up is recognizing people and situations for what they really are. The Bible talks of this. You can recognize "good" people by the good things they do just as you can recognize "bad" people by the bad things they do. You can recognize a good situation by the good outcome it brings, and you can recognize a bad situation by the bad outcome. A part of growing is to recognize and distinguish between the good and the bad.

If something smells fishy, it probably is.

"By their fruit you will recognize them … every good tree bears good fruit, but a bad tree bears bad fruit." - Matthew 7:16-17

Walking the Boardwalk

At Weko Beach the majority of people walk the sand along the water's edge. They choose the beach over the boardwalk.

We all have a calling from God. We may be called to do things others don't agree with. We are called to live a different lifestyle. It may not be what everyone else is doing, much like walking the boardwalk instead of the beach.

You are called to a life in God. No matter what that calling is, God and His ways should be a part of it. That may mean separating yourself from others who take a path God has not called you to take. One thing is for sure. The Bible says, "Blessed" is the one who follows Him.

Find joy walking your boardwalk even if you are alone. It is better than walking the beach with others.

"Blessed is the one who does not walk in step with the wicked or stand in the way that sinners take, or sit in the company of mockers, but whose delight is in the law of the Lord."
— Psalms 1:1-2

Go the Distance

I am always amazed at how many cars with out-of-state license plates are in the parking lot at Weko Beach. There are a lot of Indiana and Illinois plates, but not as many Michigan ones. Many Michiganders miss out on the beautiful summer days along Lake Michigan.

People come from far away to visit Weko Beach. Some out-of-staters have second homes along Lake Michigan just to get out of the city and enjoy what we have in southwest Michigan.

How far are you willing to go to enjoy a day with God? Believe it or not, those days are special to both you and Him. The frosting on the cake, though, is that you can reach out and connect with Him wherever you are. You don't have to go to Weko Beach. You don't have to be in church. You can be right where you are and go the distance by quietly calling out to Him.

Go the distance. Enjoy the day with God.

"From the ends of the earth I call to You, I call as my heart grows faint: lead me to the rock that is higher than I." – Psalm 61:2

Linger Longer

The booth coming into Weko Beach was empty. There were fewer cars in the parking lot and fewer people on the sand. The Beach Town Grill was closed too. These were the signs that things were winding down. The season had come to an end. Stirring inside me as it does every year was the desire to linger longer and grab as much of the beach as I could before the snow blew.

We put effort into things we like. We make the time. We linger longer. We are like a beachgoer trying to grab the most out of the summer while we can.

Just as seasons come to an end, the Bible gives advice: to seek God when He can be found. Take time for church. Linger longer reading His Word. Pray. Grab the opportunities to grow closer to Him and to praise Him. Make the most out of your time with Him.

Treat today as if it were the last day of the season: Draw near to God.

"Seek the Lord while He may be found; call on Him while He is near." – Isaiah 55:6

Washed Away

As I walked along Weko Beach, I could see others had already walked there. They left behind footprints. Part of the trail they left behind had been washed away by the water.

People impact our lives whether we want them to or not. They leave their mark. Hopefully most of it is positive, but we all probably have at least one person who has left an unwanted mark on us. Even the Bible talks of lives and decisions affecting future generations to come.

You may not always want or invite those unwanted footprints into the story of your life, but God can wash them away just as Lake Michigan washes away the footprints left behind by earlier beachgoers. He does that with His own Good News: Jesus. Jesus lived a perfect life and died not only for your sins but for the unwanted turns in life and the uninvited pain left by others. His death and resurrection give hope. It takes away the pain and the power of the mistakes others leave on your life. Jesus washes it all away.

"He leads me besides quiet waters, He refreshes my soul." – Psalms 23:2-3

Walking on Empty

The other day I didn't find any Indian beads. I went home empty-handed, but here I was again. Another day, another walk. I might go days without finding any beads, but I would still come back to Weko Beach and walk again.

It's easy to give up when we don't see the results of our efforts. It seems pointless to try. It's at those times we can experience the essence of faith.

Faith is more than just believing things will change. It is believing *and* taking steps toward those changes until things start happening. Continue to try even when you can't see the results. Your choice to continue on becomes faith in action. You do what you can and leave the results to God.

Walking on empty leaves you full of faith.

"In the same way, faith by itself, if it is not accompanied by action, is dead."
- James 2:17

Tossed Sand

My eyes watered uncontrollably as I tried to get the sand out of them. I understood why my mom taught us not to throw sand. It hurts when it gets in our eyes. I sat there hoping my tears would wash away the hurt.

We can live our lives right and follow all the rules, but don't be fooled. Even if we do everything right, there will be problems. There will be hurts. We can't control other people. They can throw the sand even when we don't, and it may get in our eyes and not theirs. It doesn't seem fair.

Jesus spoke of troubles in this life. Some people give up on Him because troubles continue after they start following Him. You can't escape them, but with Jesus you overcome them. Just as the tears cleared away the sand tossed by someone else, Jesus can flow through you and overcome any troubles.

So when the sand hits your eyes, let the tears flow and the healing begin.

"In this world you will have trouble. But take heart! I have overcome the world."
- John 16:33

Skipping Stones

Weko Beach was calm as we looked for flat stones to skip across the smooth water. As usual it turned into a competition between my son and me to see who could get the most skips before the stone disappeared into the water.

We all have different abilities, but what we do with them is what matters. We may not pick them up and use them. We may pick them up and put them in our pocket to keep for ourselves. Or we could do what we did and skip them.

You have a choice. Will you leave your abilities unused like a skipping stone on the beach? Will you keep your abilities for yourself and stuff them in your pocket? Or will you choose to skip them? Every time you choose to use your abilities in God's way, it's like skipping a stone back into the water. It's giving back to God what He gave you. It's choosing life, not leaving abilities unused or hidden.

Skip your stone across the water and see what God does.

"Now choose life, so that you and your children may live." - Deuteronomy 30:19

Surrounded by Sea Gulls

The sea gulls surrounded me and reminded me of that phrase, "Birds of a feather flock together." It occurred to me that I was nothing like them and yet here I was surrounded by them.

Sometimes we find ourselves with a group of people wondering why we are there and feeling like we don't fit in. We are the odd birds out in the feathered group of birds.

Has this ever happened to you? There may be reasons for this. Maybe you really don't fit in and that may not be a bad thing. The Bible tells us bad company corrupts good character. Growing up means recognizing who will have a good influence on you and who won't. It means making choices to bring out the good character God has placed in you. It means choosing those friends who encourage your walk with Him—those who value God and their relationship with Him as you do.

Stick with birds of the same feather.

"Do not be misled: bad company corrupts good character." - 1 Corinthians 15:33

The Real Foundation

"Do I trust this boardwalk? It's built in sand. Sand is shifty and not as solid like clay or dirt." That's what I was thinking the first time I headed up the tallest boardwalk at Weko Beach. Could I trust it? The farther I walked up the boardwalk, the more confident I felt about its structure.

Many of us work. It's part of our calling. We learn and study whatever our work requires. We become confident and sure of ourselves. The farther we get into it, the more we learn and rely on what we know and what we can do.

I trusted in the boardwalk that first day I climbed it. But really my trust should have been in its foundation. It's the same with your life. Your life's calling is not what holds you up. Jesus does. Don't build your life's foundation on what you do or what you know. Build on the real foundation— Jesus.

Don't trust in the boardwalk. Trust in the Foundation.

"For no one can lay any foundation other than the one already laid, which is Jesus Christ."
- 1 Corinthians 3:11

Beach Runner

I'm not a runner. Years ago, I tried. I ran at the local high school or along the neighborhood roads. I also tried running along Weko Beach. It offered beautiful scenery and seemed like a picture-perfect place to run, but it's hard to run on sand. It's not as solid a footing as pavement.

It's not easy living life God's way … a lot like running on a sandy beach. His way means we run from the things we naturally want. The things He wants us to run after tend to fall to the bottom of the list. Things like doing things right, living out faith, loving, and being peace-makers. These things are easily forgotten in the day-to-day run of life. They are hard to measure, and we never feel like we are on solid ground when pursuing them but …

Be a beach runner anyway. The water is right there when you need it.

"Flee the evil desires of youth and pursue righteousness, faith, love, and peace, along with those who call on the Lord out of a pure heart."
- 2 Timothy 2:22

Dark Woods

Walking along the water's edge, I looked over to the trees sitting farther back from Lake Michigan. The leaves had fallen off leaving only the dark woods. It was almost scary. I was thankful and glad to be walking near the water where things were lighter and felt safer.

As seasons of our lives come and go, so do the circumstances we find ourselves in. There are times we are in light safe areas. There are also dark scary times like the dark woods set back along Weko Beach.

During those dark scary times you don't have to be afraid. You don't have to worry. There is comfort. Jesus walks with you all the time. He is the light of the world lighting your way in the darkest of circumstances. Even when you find yourself in the middle of the dark woods …

Jesus lights the way.

"I am the light of the world. Whoever follows Me will never walk in darkness but will have the light of life." - John 8:12

Powerful Cigar Boats

As I walk along the beach, I sometimes see these powerful "cigar" boats. You can't miss them. Their engines scream with power as they fly across Lake Michigan.

If we are honest with ourselves, there are days when we scream with power and gusto like nothing can stop us or get in our way. Other days, not so much. We feel helpless and so inept with whatever we are going through. We don't have the power like those big cigar boats racing through the water.

On those days you feel so out of control and unable to handle whatever you face, you have a source of power to turn to, more powerful than screaming cigar boats: God. He made the cigar boats and the water they race through. He made you. He knows about each and every situation. He knows and has the power to handle them even when you don't.

Trust in God. His power is greater than the cigar boats on Lake Michigan.

"Is anything too hard for the Lord?"
- Genesis 18:14

Not Just for the Young

I must have walked right by the Indian bead laying in the sand in front of me. I could still see the footprints I left earlier. How could I have missed it?

It's not until we grow older that we become more aware of the plight of the elderly. Products seem to be geared around younger people and families unless it has something to do with dentures or life insurance ... The older generations are considered to be at a disadvantage because they haven't kept up with the times or current trends. It's as if a full and blessed life is over after a certain age.

That's what the world would have you believing, but God tells you differently. Both young and old have their blessings whether in their strength or in their length of days. Just as I found my bead at the end of my walk, you can find blessings in your later years. God doesn't bestow all the blessings He has for you only in your youth. He saves some for your older years too. Blessings are not just for the young.

"The glory of young men is their strength, gray
hair the splendor of the old."
- Proverbs 20:29

Wet Footprints

The footprints were defined. I could see the size and shape of the person's foot much better than the footprints left in the dry sand.

What do we want people to think of us when life is over? We can leave a good impression where they will know our beliefs and what we lived for defined by the way we lived our lives with God's guidance. Or they will remember the bad impressions we leave behind.

Just as wet sand is needed to make a good footprint, the good impression you want to leave on others needs God. He gives you a new heart and a new spirit to accomplish good things.

Walk in the wet sand ... it leaves a better footprint.

"I will give you a new heart and put a new spirit in you." - Ezekiel 36:26

All in the Timing

The flat stone I tried to skip got lost in the choppy water. On days like this, it's hard to skip stones. The toss has to be done at just the right time so the stone skips over each wave while skimming the surface between them. Timing is everything.

We have successful and unsuccessful attempts. We may think we are well-prepared and fully able to handle what we are about to tackle, but things don't work out the way we envisioned. We have all it takes and yet it still doesn't work. It's much like skipping stones on choppy water. If the timing isn't right, it's going nowhere.

There is a time for everything. A time to gather your stones and a time to toss them ... a time to develop your abilities and a time to use them ... a time for things to work and a time when things don't work. God is the only One able to put all the different aspects together perfectly.

It's all in the timing—God's timing.

"There is a time for everything, and a season for every activity under the heavens ... a time to scatter stones and a time to gather them."
- Ecclesiastes 3:1, 5

Balancing Act

The others moved around on two feet when they weren't flying in the air, but this sea gull stood on one leg. I think he was sleeping. How could he stay so perfectly balanced while asleep? Awake, I couldn't even be so balanced.

We run this way and that. We load our days with tons of things to do and then add more on. We complain. We go about our busyness, inwardly wanting peace and some sense of balance to our lives.

The first time I thought about Proverbs 11:1, I pictured a farmer weighing out produce to sell on a scale and thought it only had to do with selling fair and accurate amounts of produce. But really God loves true balance whether it has to do with selling goods or living life. Too much effort, too much commitment to someone or something may be a symptom God is not where He should be in your life. But, be encouraged. If God can give balance to a sleeping sea gull standing on one foot, He can and will give you the balance you need in your life too.

"The Lord detests dishonest scales, but accurate weights find favor with Him."
- Proverb 11:1

Sandy Boardwalks

I started along the boardwalk thinking I could avoid the sand, but to my dismay it drifted over the boardwalk. In those areas, I couldn't see the wood under my feet.

It's hard sometimes for us to know what God is calling us to do. We can't make heads or tails of it. It's hidden from us. It's almost as if life covers up our calling just like the sand covers the boardwalk. We can't see the next step.

You will have times in life when you don't know what to do next. It may be buried in the sand. I looked farther ahead and was able to tell where the boardwalk led. When you don't know the next step look farther, deeper into the Word. Jesus shows the way. His life and His Word show the next steps for today when you can't see them.

Sand may cover your boardwalk but follow the Way and you will stay on track.

"So how can we know the way?"
- John 14:5

Better Together

I see them every day I walk. They are couples. They are families. They are moms or dads with children. They are friends. They are people walking Weko Beach together.

We can't go through life without people. Most of us have family or a few close friends we go through life with. It's like walking the beach together.

There are good reasons to have others around. Hebrews 10 tells us a few of those reasons. People can stir you up and on to love and to do good. They can point you in the right direction and keep you headed that way. They can lift you up and encourage you through tough times. They are the ones doing life together with you—taking time out for you and you for them.

Take a walk with someone. It's better together.

"And let us consider how we may spur one another on toward love and good deeds, not giving up meeting together but encouraging one another." - Hebrews 10:24-25

February

"What's a boardwalk if no one walked it but you?"

Wet Sand

Have you ever been to the beach on a windy day? The wind blows the dry sand, and it stings as it hits your legs. The wet sand stands firmly grounded in spite of the wind.

How many times do we give in and not stand our ground? We give into things we probably shouldn't give into and do things we really don't want to do. We are like dry sand blown this way and that with whatever wind of circumstance stirs at the time.

Jesus offers you living water, bringing you real life full of directed purpose and the ability to stay on course. He is the water wetting your dry life and keeping it together. He gives you the strength to stand your ground when the winds start blowing.

A life soaked in the Living Water is not easily blown away.

"I thirst for You, my whole being longs for You, in a dry and parched land where no water is."
– Psalm 63:1

Moving Right Along

My eyes zeroed in on an Indian bead laying in the sand in front of me. I bent down, picked it up, and put it in my pocket. Then I continued walking along the beach until the next one was found. That was how my collection of beads started.

Finding Indian beads is much like finding the blessings God has in store for us. When I found a bead, I picked it up. I spent a little time focused on it, but not long. Then I moved along. His blessings are like that.

Enjoy your blessings from God, but there comes a time to move along. He has more blessings to show you. You restrict God when you limit your blessings only to what He has already given you. Keep on walking and keep on looking for the next one. God knows your paths. He knows when and where to place the next blessing. You just need to bend down, pick it up, and then move along.

"I press on toward the goal to win the prize for which God has called me heavenward in Christ."
- Philippians 3:14

Buried in Sand

I passed a family on Weko Beach burying one of their own in the sand. The young boy laid still and barked out instructions to his sister. He seemed to be enjoying his predicament.

Life brings many different experiences. There may be activities that are just okay and others we really enjoy.

Do you sometimes feel guilty about enjoying something? Maybe you believe you are not living right if you aren't working or sacrificing for others. Life includes work and sacrifice, but there is more to it than that. God wants you to enjoy the life He has given you. You don't have to feel guilty about it.

You can be like the boy in the sand … burying yourself in it without feeling bad.

"There is nothing better for people than to be happy. This is the gift of God."
– Ecclesiastes 3:12-13

Stony Openings

Once the sand was molded into place for my sandcastle, I would add details. Those details would come in the form of small pieces of driftwood or stones or whatever else I could find. Stones the right size and shape would define the doors and windows. Other stones would be used for stony bridges over the moat surrounding the castle.

Some days we wonder if we have what it takes to handle our life and all the curve balls thrown our way. We can see only part of the solutions to our dilemmas. It can be scary.

But God has everything you need to deal with life. You may already have it. You may find it as you go along, or maybe you need to start thinking outside the box. Just as I used a stone to build part of my castle, God gives abilities to build up your life and the lives of those around you.

Imagine what your abilities can do. God has already provided.

"His divine power has given us everything we need for a godly life." - 2 Peter 1:3

Distinguishing Flies

My husband and I sat on beach towels looking out over the water. I was enjoying the sights and sounds of our young kids playing in the water, unaware of the flies relentlessly biting my husband as I sat unbothered next to him.

Isn't it odd how flies can bite the person right next to you and not bother you at all? A similar event happened in the Old Testament. God sent a swarm of flies as one of the ten plagues. This plague was different. Up until the flies, the plagues affected everyone. Now the flies bothered only the Egyptians, distinguishing them from the Israelites.

God has the ability to deal differently with each one of us. The Bible records why He did this—to let the Egyptians know He is God and He was watching over His people.

Distinguishing flies reminds us of the presence and power of God.

"I will deal differently with the land of Goshen.
No swarm of flies will be there, so that you will
know that I, the Lord, am in this land."
— Exodus 8:22

Lonely Boardwalks

There was no one except me on the boardwalk. There was no one to pass by and no one to scoot out of the way for. I was alone.

We live in a world of people. It's not just us and aren't we thankful for that! Our calling is about others and how Jesus can use us.

If you look at Jesus, He spent His life healing and teaching. Many places in the Bible, we read how He reached out and touched those He came to help. He touched the lives of others and it made all the difference in the world to them. Your calling in life will take you places where you can reach out and touch the lives of those around you.

What's a boardwalk if no one walked it but you?

"But Jesus came and touched them. 'Get up', He said. 'Don't be afraid.'" — Matthew 17:7

Texting

On occasion I laugh to myself about my texting. You see, I text ideas and thoughts to myself as I walk along Lake Michigan. I laugh at what others may be thinking … "She can't even put her phone down long enough for a walk on the beach." They don't know I'm texting myself.

We may not want to admit it, but we often judge others by what we see. We go no further than that. We don't know all the circumstances surrounding other people's decisions. We don't know what's really going on inside. But we judge just the same.

Isn't it wonderful to have a God who sees everything? He sees what you do outwardly and understands why and how you got there. Understanding can play an important role when watching someone's actions. It's a way of looking at things from the inside. God not only understands, but He still loves us even knowing what we are on the inside.

Got a word from God today? Send yourself a text.

"You are judging by appearances."
— 2 Corinthians 10:7

Unseasonably Warm

People were coming out of their homes to the beach as if winter hibernation was over. It was almost 60 degrees in February, unseasonably warm for the harsh winter season.

When we go through difficult times, peace is hard to come by. We go through day after day, facing harsh circumstances. We want a break like an unseasonably warm day on the beach in the middle of winter.

Wouldn't a break from our problems be nice? As I struggled through tough problems, I went through days without a break. I experienced something ... the only way to describe it ... I was at peace. The problems weren't worked out and I didn't even have the answers. What I had was the simple fact that however the situation turned out, I was ok because God was in control. Whatever He worked out I knew I would be ok. That is God's peace ... different from the world's peace. Peace not based on circumstances or answers. He is your unseasonably warm day in the middle of hard winters.

"Peace I leave with you; My peace I give you. I do not give to you as the world gives." - John 14:27

Shaken by a Wake

The lake is calm. No waves. Nothing but smooth sailing. It's the kind of day to get on your air mattress and float peacefully on the water. Then, a boat goes by and the calm water disappears as the waves begin to splash over the air mattress, interrupting your peace.

It reminds me of a time in my life when my faith seemed to be shaken. Life was calm and peaceful until that day. What happened caused me to question God and what I believe about Him.

We all have times when our faith is shaken. Even the daily news can cause us to question God. But the Bible tells us to hold fast to Him. He is faithful. I chose to put my trust in God, to believe He cares, to believe He sees, to believe He is able, and to believe He will make things right. I had to wait but it came.

Don't let the wake shake your faith. Hold on.

"Let us hold unswervingly to the hope we profess, for He who promised is faithful."
- Hebrews 10:23

Among the Stones

I walked through the span of stones along the beach. I don't really like to do that because they are hard on my feet, but it paid off. I found another bead. I decided to continue on since more Indian beads can be found in the stones.

We find ourselves living through difficult circumstances or maybe with difficult people. It's not always fun or easy and we may not like it. Our lives may seem harder than the lives of others around us and it may very well be.

Some of my greatest blessings were found in the most difficult times of my life. It's was in those difficult times that my faith grew the most and I was defining who I was with every tough decision I made. A stronger faith and being who you are ... are blessings. You may have a choice to move over to the softer sand—to make life easier—but with that choice blessings may be missed.

Are you willing to walk among the stones?

"Blessed is the one who perseveres under trial because, having stood the test, that person will receive the crown of life." - James 1:12

Uneven Walk

Walking in uneven sand can be hard. Good solid steps give way as the sand moves under the pressure. It's not easy-going like walking on smooth, hard, even pavement.

Isn't it hard to walk through life sometimes? We struggle to keep our balance. We may not know how to move forward and, even if we do, it still can be a struggle.

I imagine Jesus as He carried the cross and the struggles He had. The cross was probably heavy and the road uneven. He struggled, but He kept going. He carried His cross along an uneven road and set the example for us.

When life gets hard and you start struggling … when things seem unfair and you are carrying the greater load, keep on the uneven path. Jesus did, and He is there along the way to help.

Walk in the uneven sands of life just as Jesus did.

"Carrying His own cross, He went out to the place of the Skull." - John 19:17

Big Stones

My kids and I decided to see who could toss a stone the farthest into Lake Michigan. I picked up a small stone and tossed it. My daughter picked up a stone and tossed it. My son, well, he struggled. He tossed it and it fell into the water not far from him. He chose a big heavy stone.

Don't we get caught up thinking bigger is better? We idolize athletes who make it professionally. We idolize the rich who have everything money can buy. But just as my son's bigger rock didn't go very far, sometimes bigger doesn't go so far either.

Your small abilities can go farther than the big abilities someone else has. It's all in how you choose to use them. In the Bible, God used small, insignificant people to make great differences. It's not the size of your abilities that matters, but Who guides your use of them.

God determines what is better and what is more effective.

"For My thoughts are not your thoughts, neither are your ways My ways." - Isaiah 55:8

Barefoot in February

The unseasonably warm day in the middle of February drew a crowd at Weko Beach. People were here to enjoy the day as if winter were once again on the run. I enjoyed following a set of footprints in the sand. The warm day set us free from the harsh cold winter.

God is like that. He sets us free in the middle of cold, harsh seasons of our lives. We find peace, joy, and confidence in difficult times when we should have worry, sadness, and fear. We don't have to worry about doing things the world's way. We don't have to worry about what others think. God has a way of setting us free from all that. When He shows us the direction for the situation we find ourselves in, we find confidence in following Him. There is peace and joy in knowing that we are obediently being led by Him. No other person's opinion can diminish our freedom when its source is from God.

Gods sets us free to go barefoot in February.

"Where the Spirit of the Lord is, there is freedom." - 2 Corinthians 3:17

Surfacing Fish

In the early evenings, I've seen little ripples on top of Lake Michigan where small fish come to the surface of the water to get food or a breath of fresh air.

We get stuck in the mundane and run ourselves ragged. We need replenishment. We need to catch our breath. We need to be restored, refreshed.

There is no better answer to burnout and mundane times than Christ. He offers you renewed, restored, and refreshed life through the encouragement and hope found in His Word. His Word guides you each day rightly through difficult circumstances. His Word reminds you of His great love for you. His Word helps you succeed. His Word lets you enjoy the simple things in life. You've grown when you realize your need for Christ and you go to Him daily for His Word.

Be a fish. Come up for Bread. Come up for a breath of fresh air.

"Give us today our daily bread."
- Matthew 6:11

Bench Break

Along the boardwalks are benches. Walk a ways and find yet another one. You don't have to go far without a place to sit and take a break.

Hard work is respectable, but don't we sometimes treat work as if it is the most important thing in the world? We work long hours. We come into work during our time off or we may even skip vacations altogether. We feel so admirable because of our over-commitment to work.

There is nothing wrong with hard work but, like everything else, it needs to be kept in perspective. Jesus understands the need for a break. He often took time away. He even offers you rest. God exhibited a need for a break when He took the seventh day off from His creative work. Just as there are benches along the boardwalk to take a break, you need to take breaks from your calling. It's a way to refresh yourself and gain a new perspective.

Go ahead … sit on the bench and take a break.

"Come to Me, all you who are weary and burdened, and I will give you rest."
– Matthew 11:28

Benchwarmers

I call them "benchwarmers." They tend to be the older generations sitting on the wooden benches facing the water. When I was younger, I didn't envy them at all. They were wasting precious time at the beach. Me, on the other hand, I was there to get the most out of it. I'm older now ...

We go about life trying to get the most out of it. We rush here and there doing whatever we think will make us happy. We are busy playing the game like a member of the starting line up in the game of life. We aren't benchwarmers.

Maybe the benchwarmers at Weko Beach got it right ... sitting on a bench facing the water and just delighting in it. It's like sitting in the presence of God and just enjoying it. No rushing about trying to play the game.

Be a benchwarmer in the presence of God.

"Take delight in the Lord, and He will give you the desires of your heart." - Psalm 37:4

Die-Hard Beachgoers

Labor Day is the last official day of the summer season. After the weekend holiday, there aren't as many beachgoers. It becomes even fewer as the snow starts to fall. Those few are the die-hard beachgoers. They are there no matter what.

We don't always like what we hear. Some turn away from the Bible and church, thinking it's full of too many do's and don'ts they don't want to follow. God's Word may be difficult for some to swallow so they walk away much like a beachgoer walking away from the beach when the snow starts to blow.

What do you do when you hear things from God's Word you don't really want to hear let alone follow? Many disciples turned away from Jesus. They wouldn't accept what He talked about. Sometimes you just have to accept that He is Lord. He sees and knows what you don't. Accept Him at His Word even if it isn't what you want to hear and even if becomes difficult.

Will you be a die-hard follower?

"From this time many of His disciples turned back and no longer followed Him." - John 6:66

Healing Water

My heart hurt and my mind was numb. I was in the midst of a struggle bringing me to the lowest point in my life. Here on Weko Beach, I just walked. I kept walking.

Pure water can be very healing and good for people. My walks were like taking a fresh sip of healthy, clean water. It was like bathing in pure water. My walks helped me wash away the ugliness I was going through and the ugliness of how I was handling it.

I didn't have pure, fresh water in reality there. The pure, fresh water I had was God who walked with me on the beach encouraging and guiding me, telling me I was loved in the midst of everything. He was healing me as I walked.

So how do you handle your tough situations? How can you bring God into it?

God is the healing water for your soul.

"I will bring health and healing."
- Jeremiah 33:6

Dead Bones

The person struck up a conversation. "Indian beads are really dead fish bones." I already knew that but I collect them anyway. It amazes me how many things I have learned from dead fish bones.

Jesus' death teaches us too. We learn of a man turning down all the powers of heaven to die for us so we can have eternity in heaven with Him. We are instilled with hope because no matter what we face His bones are not in the grave. He is there loving and caring about us even today. He blessed us by His death.

If God can teach me using the dead bones of a fish, the fish's death was not in vain. When you live a life committed to Jesus, you do not die in vain. Your life will leave memories, and who knows how God will use your death to speak to others?

Even in death, God can still use you to bless others.

"But God demonstrates His own love for us in this: while we were still sinners, Christ died for us." - Romans 5:8

Beginning of Change

The walks along Weko Beach are different from year to year. Not by much, but they are different. I find myself taking note of the differences each new spring. One notable difference is where the sand stops and the water starts.

Our lives change over time. There are times we welcome the change and other times we don't. It can make us nervous and we feel out of control.

Change began with God. He initiated it from the beginning and He is still the initiator today. When He created the world saying, "Let there be …" He was initiating change—a whole new world. He looked at it and saw that it was good.

When life changes, you may not always welcome it. One thing is for sure, God who in His unmeasurable power spoke change into being is powerful enough to handle the changes in your life.

Trust God. Change begins with Him.

"And God said, 'Let there be.'"
- Genesis 1:3

Piled Up and Unused

I walked by a pile of stones in the sand. They obviously had been gathered by someone and left there. As a child, I gathered a bunch of stones for whatever I was doing. When it came time to leave, the stones were left on the beach in a pile and unused.

We may handle our abilities differently. Some may take full advantage of what they can do, while others take it for granted.

The Bible has a parable about the use of talents. A man gave "talents" of differing amounts to different people so they could use them for good. They all used their talents wisely except for one who buried his "talent" and hid it. He didn't use it, but instead tried to give it back exactly as he had received it—much like collecting stones and leaving them on the beach unused. God gives you talent and He expects you to do something with it. It's not enough to return your talent exactly as you received it.

Will you leave your stones on the beach unused?

"Well done, good and faithful servant."
- Matthew 25:23

Different World

In the most difficult times of my life, I took time away from the problems coming down on me and escaped to Weko Beach. I walked with God in my own little world where I found peace, answers, hope, and love that seemed so hard to find in those difficult days.

We have times in our lives where we want to escape it all. The pressures and responsibilities are too much. The painful circumstances threaten our lives and maybe even our well-being.

God offers you refuge, a place of solitude, a place to sort things out, to encourage, and to remember His strength and love. Real growth recognizes your places of refuge. It recognizes where you tune into God best whether it is sitting on a church pew, kneeling next to your bed, or even walking on a beach.

God's refuge takes you to a whole different world.

"God is our refuge and strength."
- Psalm 46:1

Stubborn Boardwalks

As people walk along Lake Michigan, the sand changes and a footprint is left. They leave their mark. Not so with the boardwalk. People can walk the boardwalk, but it doesn't change. It remains the same as it was before.

Life brings changes. It did in mine and, if I am honest, I didn't always want those changes. It was during one of those times, I learned to stand my ground. It didn't matter what was thrown at me; I was going to go for what I wanted—what I thought was right. I became stubborn in my commitment and my calling.

Have you ever faced a situation that threatened to tear down your commitments, pushing you to give up your calling? You can be stubborn about it just like a boardwalk refusing to give way when stepped all over. When you commit to the righteous ways God approves of, you learn to be stubborn for His way of life and what He meant it to be. Commitment to God and His ways should never cave in.

Be stubborn no matter how much you get walked on.

"Commit to the Lord whatever you do, and He will establish your plans." – Proverb 16:3

Private Beach

I tried walking north along Weko Beach. I didn't get too far. A "Private Beach" sign stopped me. The sign kept out beachgoers who didn't live on the lake.

We probably all have run into those "Private Beach" signs—people building walls around themselves shutting us out and making it difficult to get to know them or be a part of their lives.

The Bible tells how the Israelites conquered Jericho. It started with bringing the walls down. How? By marching around it. They were instructed by God and followed His lead in faith until the walls fell down. If you are facing "Private Beach" signs, do what the Israelites did:

Follow God in faith until the sign falls down.

"By faith the walls of Jericho fell, after the army had marched around them for seven days."
- Hebrews 11:30

A New Day

A walk on Weko Beach in the spring starts it all off. The trees setting back from the shore have a hint of green from the small, barely visible buds. The sounds of the beach return—the cawing of the sea gulls and the gentle roll of the waves. Hope for the summer to come springs up inside.

We all go through cold and difficult seasons in our lives. The key word here is "through." When we go through hard times, we come out on the other side. It's a lot like returning to the beach on a spring day after a long cold hard winter.

Problems can seem insurmountable and you may think things can never change. I've been there and I can say that God restored my hope. Jesus overcame death. Don't you think He can overcome your problems too? Put your hope in Him and His resurrection.

Walk like it's a spring day.

"In His great mercy He has given us new birth into a living hope through the resurrection of Jesus Christ from the dead." - 1 Peter 1:3

Water Logged

I stood on the huge log near the water's edge and, although it rocked with the waves, I could feel the weight of it beneath my feet. It was heavy. Even if I had wanted to move it, it would have been impossible. I was not strong enough.

Why do we need God? I used to think I could handle anything that came my way, but life came and situations happened. I learned that some things in life are too hard to face alone. We need God. We need Him because we don't have the strength, whether emotionally or physically, to handle every situation on our own. He is like that powerful water we call Lake Michigan. It moves the huge, heavy logs drifting in and out of our lives. God becomes our strength in those heavy times. That is why we need Him.

It's okay to need God when you are water logged.

"But you, Lord, do not be far from me. You are my strength; come quickly to help me."
- Psalm 22:19

Camping

I like sitting around a campfire, but I'm not a camper. People leave their homes and day-to-day lives to camp. I started wondering why campers are drawn to Weko Beach. Maybe it's because of the water.

When we are drawn to something, we make choices moving in that direction. Sometimes it means giving up things. It's like the campers. They are drawn to Weko Beach giving up days of home-grown comfort to camp.

Are you drawn to God? Are you willing to give up some of the comforts you now have to be closer to Him? When you start doing things to get closer to God, He steps it up too. He promises in His Word that He will move towards you as you move towards Him. What are those things in your life that are pulling you towards God? Pursue them.

Camp if it brings you closer to Him.

"Come near to God and He will come near to you." - James 4:8

Sea Gull Army

At first, I was a little taken back. I was so wrapped up collecting Indian beads that I was unaware of the sea gulls. They lined my path next to the water and stood their ground watching me.

It's easy to be afraid when you can't see what God sees. God knows what faces you. He knows the walls you run up against and the forces coming against you. You don't have to be afraid. He always has you in His sight with His army ready at His command to protect you.

You may be like me and fear things you face, but in an effort to grow in Christ, let's together set aside our fears and anxieties, trusting in the Lord even when we can't see Him.

His army is watching over you like the sea gulls of Weko Beach.

"Those who are with us are more than those who are with them. And Elisha prayed: Open his eyes, Lord, so that he may see. Then the Lord opened the servant's eyes, and he looked and he saw the hills full of horses and chariots."
— 2 Kings 6:16-17

March

"Dig deeper to strike Water."

When Water Meets Sky

It was cloudy and a little overcast. It was one of those days when you look out over Lake Michigan and you can't tell where the water ends and the sky begins.

We have cloudy days in our lives when things aren't clear and the heaviness of what we are going through blurs our horizons. Things may not be clear to us, but they are clear to God. His authority over our lives, His wisdom, His love, and His ability is unlimited. We can't see where Lake Michigan meets the sky, but God can. "The sky's the limit" doesn't apply to Him. He has no limits.

So no matter what you are facing, smile. God's got you covered. Nothing, nothing is impossible for Him.

"Oh, the depth of the riches of the wisdom and knowledge of God! How unsearchable His judgments, and His paths beyond tracing out!"
– Romans 11:33

An Abundant Supply

I started collecting Indian beads years ago. I keep them in a jar with a cork lid. Now years later, that jar is full of nothing but Indian beads. Any size and any condition, it's there in my jar. It's an abundant supply reminding me of my many, many walks along Lake Michigan.

One day my walk brought a change in me I wasn't expecting. I realized how many beads I had and that maybe it was time for me to share them. My quest for Indian beads would never be the same.

My collection of Indian beads represented the blessings I have received from God over the years. When that jar filled up, I realized God had blessed me in so many more ways than just giving me a bead here and there. I found my life full of His goodness. People all around are going through hard times and difficult things. They need to know the blessings of God. When you recognize the abundant blessings you have from Him, it's easy to give what you have to others. I still collect Indian beads to remind me of God's blessings, but now I'm learning to give them away.

"It is more blessed to give than to receive."
— Acts 20:35

Digging for Water

When I was young, I would try to build a castle on the beach with a moat around it. I would dig deep knowing if I dug deep enough water would show up at the bottom. Sometimes I had to dig even deeper to hit water.

Life presents many opportunities to dig deeper. Whether it's to solve a problem, to find encouragement, or just because, the Bible tells us to search for God first above all else. We can go to His Word to help with the deeper issues of life.

Just like when I had to dig deeper to find water, when you dig deeper in your search for God, you find Him. It's at that point you learn more about Him and about His heart. You receive a better understanding to your problems when you understand His heart better. You find encouragement with the slightest hint of His presence and contentment in His righteous ways.

Dig deeper and you will strike Water!

"But seek first His kingdom and His righteousness, and all these things will be given to you as well." – Matthew 6:33

Don't Throw Stones

I walked past a family with young kids and listened as the mother told her son, "Don't throw stones. You might hit someone." I heard that a few times growing up and I told my own kids the same thing. If you throw stones, it could hurt someone.

We are all blessed with talents. We are given the choice on how we use them. We may choose to use them to benefit many or a few. We may choose to use them here and now or in the future. We may choose to use them in a way that brings comfort or discomfort depending on the situation. The point is we have choices to use our abilities for good or bad, to help or to hurt.

God tells you everything you do should be to build each other up. In other words, do good in all things. Use your talents to build up the lives around you (including yours). It's like that stone on the beach.

Will you throw it and hit someone, or will you use it to build a castle?

"Everything must be done so that the church may be built up." – 1 Corinthians 14:26

Basking in the Sun

The sun felt good shining down on me. I welcomed the warmth. It seemed to permeate my skin. I was not alone. Ahead was a group of sea gulls basking in the sun, enjoying it as I was.

Doesn't the sun conjure up feelings of hope on dark days? We walk through life and, on some days, we could use a little sunshine ... a little hope. We want to bask in it just as the sea gulls do on Weko Beach.

Hope comes from above. Not from heaven, not from the sun, but from God. Stay in the Word. Keep your focus on Him. When those dark days come, you will have hope. He is the giver of hope when you have none left. Let His hope permeate deep into your soul and heal your brokenness.

Bask in the Lord and find hope.

"May the God of hope fill you with all joy and peace as you trust in Him, so that you may overflow with hope by the power of the Holy Spirit." – Romans 15:13

Seeing Between the Steps

I walked up the steep steps of the boardwalk. With each step, I could see in between them. Instead of building the boardwalk steps by nailing in vertical boards, the builders left it open.

Have you ever been told you were hard to read? Some people are hard to read. We watch, we talk to them, we listen to them, and we still can't figure them out. They aren't very transparent. We can't read between the steps to figure them out.

When you commit your life to Christ, He comes and lives inside you. You begin to think like Him. You take on His heart. You love the things He loves and hate the things He hates. The things that hurt Him hurt you. The words of God prove true. He lives in you. You become transparent. People look at you and see Christ.

Seeing between the steps is a good thing.

"It is no longer I who live, but Christ lives in me."
- Galatians 2:20

Uncontainable Kids

The young kids were so excited. They threw their stuff down and eagerly ran to the edge of Lake Michigan. Their excitement was uncontainable. It burst forth into shouts of exclamations and loud laughter. Everyone on the beach could hear it. The other beachgoers reacted in their own way, but it didn't matter to the kids. In their excitement to be at the beach, they were unaware of anything else.

When was the last time you were so excited about Jesus and what He has done for you? You may go to church once a week or read your Bible daily, but where is the excitement? Where is the unrestrained joy over what He has done? We "grow up" in our faith and become like beachgoers, unexcitedly sitting on the beach.

Shout. Laugh. Be excited. Jesus has saved you from whatever you messed up on. He has saved you and can heal your scars. He offers you hope, love, and everlasting life.

You can be a joyful, uncontainable kid again.

"Shout for joy to the Lord, all the earth."
- Psalm 98:4

Winter Silence

The harshness of winter had set in. I felt the cold as I walked along the beach and heard the silence. At times, the silence was too loud. I missed hearing the waves roll, but this was a season of cold winds and frozen lakes.

As we go through tough times in our lives, it's not easy to hear God. It's hard enough to hear Him anytime let alone during the difficult times. We miss hearing Him. It's like walking the frozen beach on a cold winter day and not hearing the waves.

When you struggle with hard problems, when you pray and God seems silent, He is still there. He is like the water hidden under the frozen ice. You can't hear Him. You may not be able to see Him, but He is still there. He is not going anywhere.

God is there and, in His quietness, He still loves you.

"The Lord your God is with you. In His love, He will no longer rebuke you." – Zephaniah 3:17

Watery Eyes

When I was young, I would play in Lake Michigan. I would dive under and swim along the bottom hoping to sneak up unnoticed on my unsuspecting target. Sometimes it worked. Other times, they saw me coming and moved before I got there. The problem was that I kept my eyes closed under the water so I never saw them move.

That's sort of how life is without God. We see things the way we see them and move in that direction. We make decisions based on what we see and jump right in. The problem is that things change. With God it's different. It's like keeping your eyes wide open under water. We not only see people from a different angle, we see when they move. God helps us see people and situations differently. He knows the changes coming up and helps us see possibilities in people and situations through the watery eyes of faith.

Life with God is like diving in with your eyes wide open.

"The Lord does not look at the things people look at. People look at the outward appearance, but the Lord looks at the heart." - 1 Samuel 16:7

Enjoy the Longer Walk

I watched her pick up another piece of whatever she was collecting and put it into a bag that already seem too full. My pockets were empty. I had taken a long walk and noticed her just starting off on her own walk finding items right off the bat. It didn't seem quite fair.

Life isn't fair. We have our ideas about what is fair and what isn't. We like to blame it on sin, and that could very well be the case. What I struggle with is when God seems unfair. He may bless people we know are living by their own rules while we try to live by His rules and we come up with the short end of the stick. It doesn't seem fair.

Everything here is God's. It is His to determine who gets what and how much each day. You may have to take a longer walk before you find your blessings from God, but that is His choice. You are only a steward like everyone else.

God may make you wait. Enjoy the longer walk.

"Don't I have the right to do what I want with my own money? Or are you envious because I am generous?" - Matthew 20:15

Messy Messy

She was right of course. Messy sand from the beach gets all over things. It wasn't like going to a pool with no sand to worry about.

Life gets messy. It gets even messier when you get out there and get involved. It's like choosing between going to a pool or going to the beach. We can live life where it's not too messy or we can choose to get involved.

It's not always fun and you may not always want to get involved in the problems of life, but the good thing is that God sees and He doesn't forget. People may forget what you do to help. They may forget the sacrifices you made out of love, but God remembers. Helping in those messy situations demonstrates love. God sees and He is just. He will reward you for what you have done.

Be messy. Go to the beach!

"God is not unjust. He will not forget your work and the love you have shown." – Hebrews 6:10

Skippable Stones

I tossed the stone down. The other side of it wasn't flat enough. It takes a special kind of stone to skip on the water. It shouldn't be too heavy or, for that matter, too big. Most importantly, it has to be flat.

Don't we at times wish we could do or be something we aren't? Maybe it's to be a supermom or to be a beautiful and loved wife. Maybe it's to be the successful breadwinner or the winning coach of your child's team. Whatever the wish, we don't quite seem to have what it takes.

God did make some people to be supermoms and others to be coaches of the year. Maybe you aren't one of them, but God gives you the abilities a supermom or coach of the year doesn't have. The good thing about it all is God gave you grace to go along with the abilities you do have.

Don't have a skippable stone? Use the graceful one instead.

"We have different gifts, according to the grace given to each of us." - Romans 12:6

Grass in the Sand

Even though it was grass growing on a beach, it always seemed out of place to me. I'm used to the soft plush green grass of a Michigan yard that grows well in clay soil. Nothing seems like it could really grow well in sand. Yet beach grass grows here.

We may find ourselves looking at our surroundings and questioning our circumstances. We wonder how we can grow where we are at. We feel like grass growing in the sand.

Remember Moses leading the Israelites in the desert? He hit a rock and God brought forth water for the thirsty people. If God can do that then, He can do it now. Your circumstances don't intimidate Him. He can touch whatever situation you are in and cause things to grow. He can cause you to learn and grow wherever you are at.

God can make grass grow in hot dry sand.

"He turned the desert into pools of water and the parched ground into flowing springs."
- Psalm 107:35

Graffiti

I sat on a bench in the rest area at the top of the boardwalk. It was apparent others had been this way with all the graffiti etched in the wood. It was the usual graffiti, but one caught my eye: "Love God."

As we go about our daily lives trying to fulfill our calling, it says something to those around us. Maybe we grumble about what we have on our plate. Maybe we hum a tune as we go about things. Maybe we fall asleep on the job. Or maybe we work as best we can with what sits in front of us.

It's hard to believe that what you do says anything, but people watch and they wonder. How do you show your commitment to God in the environment you are called to? Maybe it's in honesty. Maybe it's in compassion. Maybe it's through encouragement and hope. It could be in excellent work or not taking part in gossip. No matter what you do, you leave an impression much like the graffiti etched in the boardwalk's wood.

What does your graffiti say?

"But what about you? ... Who do you say I am?"
- Mark 8:29

Splash Attacks

    I backed away. I wasn't used to the water. I wasn't ready yet and usually that's when it would happen … splash attacks. I would be forced to splash back at my assailant. It would go on until one of us backed off or we called a truce.

    We all face attacks threatening our health, our jobs, our ways of life, our beliefs. We aren't ready for them and we don't really want to deal with them, but they still come like water splashing at us when we are just getting used to it.

    God is important. The Bible is important. Why? God through His Word shows you how to fight against whatever you are up against. Ephesians 6:11-17 tells you the Word of God enables you to stand against the schemes of satan. It's interesting. The weapon in splash attacks is water. God is like the water. God and His Word are our weapons.

    Fight with Water.

"Put on the full armor of God, so that you can take your stand against the devil's schemes."
- Ephesians 6:11

The Obvious

Well, it was obvious there would be no Indian beads in my path today. I didn't expect any. It was midwinter. Lake Michigan was frozen over, and the sand was covered in snow. The water would not deliver new beads, nor could it retreat leaving any behind.

Don't we expect God to deliver? We constantly look for the good we can get out of every situation, even the harshest ones. It's much like expecting an Indian bead in the dead of winter.

It's not always so obvious why God doesn't allow some blessings. You may struggle and pray. You may have reasoned it all out why getting that certain blessing makes all the sense in the world, and logically you may be right, but God still does not deliver. You may be in one of those seasons where a heavenly purpose is being worked out—a purpose no human mind can understand.

No beads? Look to heaven for the obvious.

"There is a time for everything, and a season for every activity under the heavens."
- Ecclesiastes 3:1

Safe Waters

I love dogs. Most days when I walk on Weko Beach, there is a least one beachgoer with a dog. Some ignore you while others are eager to say hello to every person walking by. Still others leave me wondering if I should keep on course. Hoping the owners control their dog, I move forward. But even that isn't enough assurance. I find myself walking deeper in the water. For some reason, I feel safer in the water than on the beach.

We have a place to go when we don't feel safe—when tough situations come and we feel insecure. The Bible tells us that God is our refuge and strength. He gives us a place to go when scary things happen. He gives us the strength to deal with it too. I went to the water, my refuge, when passing the scary dogs and stayed on course.

Where will you walk in troubled times? Will it be in the safe Water?

"God is our refuge and strength, an ever-present help in trouble." - Psalm 46:1

Ready Answers

A young boy stopped me to ask what I was collecting. He saw me bend over and pick up something before I walked past him and his family on the beach. Curiosity must have gotten the best of him, so I showed him the Indian bead I had just found without going into it much further.

Opportunities to talk of God and what He is and has been doing in our lives present themselves to us. Sometimes they come unexpectedly. We address them, probably not realizing the full extent of the opportunity in front of us.

In hind sight I wanted the opportunity all along, but I didn't realize it when it came along. I wasn't ready to tell this young boy about my collection and why it was so much more to me than collecting Indian beads. Are you ready to talk about what God means to you and why? Now is the time. Be prepared.

What will you say about your walks?

"Preach the Word; be prepared in season and out of season." - 2 Timothy 4:2

Limitless Sand

This is the first devotional I have ever written. I worried whether I would have enough to write as I walked along the beach. I looked at the sand ... so much sand.

God tells us His thoughts towards us are like the sand. Too many to count. Too many to run out. I always thought it strange that the word "thoughts" was used here. But "thoughts" could be interpreted as thoughts of encouragement, love, guidance, or maybe even as lessons.

You don't have to worry whether God has what it takes to help you through whatever you are going through. He has unlimited ways to encourage, unlimited expressions of love, unrestrained guidance, and lesson after lesson for you. Just as I didn't have to worry about God providing me ideas for this book, you don't have to worry about Him providing you what you need to face what you face. His "thoughts" are as endless as the sand.

"How precious to me are Your thoughts, God! How vast is the sum of them! Were I to count them, they would outnumber the grains of sand."
- Psalm 139:17

Keep Off

Spray painted on the stone breakers sprawling out into Lake Michigan, were the words "Keep Off." These words were sprayed there for the safety of the beachgoers. People still go out on them, ignoring the warning.

There may be things we simply can't do and other things we simply don't believe we can do. Maybe it's because we have heard somebody say too many times that we didn't have what it takes. We didn't have the skills. We didn't have the knowledge. We didn't have that magic touch. Maybe that somebody was you. It was like they were saying, "Keep Off. Don't go there. You don't have what it takes."

When someone tells me I can't, I personally find it hard to accept, especially without trying for myself. The Bible is full of truth. The truth is that when we put the outcome in Jesus' hands, He can make the impossible possible for you. It doesn't take skill, knowledge, or the magic touch. It takes reliance on Jesus. Overcome boundaries by relying on Him.

"Who is it that overcomes the world? Only the one who believes that Jesus is the Son of God."
- 1 John 5:5

Ignoring the Sign

I found it comical as I walked past the breakers near the north end of Weko Beach. Right next to the painted words "Keep Off" sat a sea gull totally ignoring the warning.

When we are young our parents and teachers—those with authority over us—guide us and teach us. We don't always understand the reasoning of their decisions, so we may ignore them and their words of wisdom. We are like the sea gull sitting on the breaker ignoring the "Keep Off" sign.

Even as an adult you can be guilty of the same thing. God's Word is full of wisdom and yet it gets ignored. His Word teaches you to say No to wrong things that could hurt or endanger you. It teaches you wisdom and self-control. You grow when you choose to stay in the Word and not ignore it.

There's nothing comical about ignoring the wisdom of God.

"It teaches us to say NO to ungodliness and worldly passions, and to live self-controlled, upright and godly lives in this present age."
- Titus 2:12

Hidden Plumbing

I found it interesting that a steel sanitation water cap was in the boardwalk closest to Lake Michigan. Why? The lake—tons of water—was only a few hundred feet away and yet the need for underground plumbing existed even there.

We can go anywhere in life, but we still need God. There isn't one place we won't need Him. There may be times when others might think it inappropriate to haul out the Bible and start reading. It might even get awkward. How can we take God with us wherever we go so we are ready to do whatever He calls us to do?

Memorizing and meditating. When you need a pick-me-up, the Bible verse you memorized is right there in your head. You don't have to flaunt it. You don't have to pull out your Bible, making you seem self-righteous. It's done quietly inside for only you and God to know. It's like having hidden plumbing under the boardwalk connecting you to that greater Water.

Pick a Bible verse and memorize it today.

"Blessed is the one …who meditates on His law day and night." - Psalms 1:1-2

Simple Hellos

It was a busy day at Weko Beach. I passed many beachgoers walking along the shore enjoying the summer day. I have learned to say hello as I pass by. Most welcome the friendly gesture and say hi back.

We never know what others around us are facing. For most people, the pain and shame of hurts and failures are things we hide. Problems are buried within. I have been there. People go to the beach for many reasons. I went to escape the pain and to sort out difficult problems.

Jesus told a parable of a Samaritan willing to help while others walked on by. You may not know what someone near you is going through, but a smile and a simple hello may be all that someone needs. It's like choosing to be the Good Samaritan. It may mean the world to someone. It did to me.

Say hello.

"And when he saw the other man, he passed by on the other side. But a Samaritan went to him."- Luke 10:31-34

Lost Kayaks

Something was missing. I couldn't quite figure it out until the end of my walk. The kayaks on the beach were missing, along with the white canopy covering them and the sign advertising their availability for rent. They must have shut down shop for the winter.

It's easy to get used to what we have as if it will always be there. Things will always be the same. Then something changes. A loved one dies. A job is lost. Our health declines. We don't understand it and we get upset, maybe even angry, with God. It's as if we expect the kayaks to stay when they are out of season.

I learned when my mother-in-law died that God has a purpose even in our losses. My mother-in-law was a cornerstone of support for my marriage. After she died and I lost that support, I turned to God more. My point is that God may take some blessings out of your life. It may hurt. The blessings may be a loss. But God still has a purpose. Don't turn away from Him. Instead, bless His name even in the loss.

"The Lord gave and the Lord has taken away; may the name of the Lord be praised." - Job 1:21

Swim above the Pebbles

Like most people, I have tender feet and it hurts to walk on the pebbles at the beach. Even the pebbles under the water hurt my feet, but the nice thing is that I can swim over them instead of walking on them.

In the Old Testament, Moses instructed the Israelites. He taught them laws to follow and spoke of the importance of following God. He told them to walk with God so they could live and things would go well with them.

Swimming over the pebbles is sort of like walking with God. He helps us with the hurtful walks in life. Instead of walking through life on our own, we can choose to swim through it with God. He eases our burdens and lets us rise above them.

Choose a better way. Swim above the pebbles.

"Walk in obedience to all that the Lord your God has commanded you, so that you may live and prosper." - Deuteronomy 5:33

Different Collections

I collect Indian beads. That's my thing. Other beachgoers collect other things. I've met people along Weko Beach who collect glass, drift wood, Petoskey rocks, shells, and sand. There are even people with metal detectors looking for hidden treasures under the sand. You name it, there is probably someone collecting it.

I think of Indian beads as blessings. I learn about God as I search for them. One day I may be reminded about His love for me and the next about His strength or how He wants me to handle whatever I am going through. The other beachgoers aren't missing out on that. They may be learning through their own collections.

I guess my point is … just as my collection of Indian beads has taught me about God, other collections may teach others about Him as well. There are many different ways to Jesus, but only one way to the Father.

What helps you find Jesus?

"No one comes to the Father except through Me." - John 14:6

Leave the Water's Edge

I didn't want to walk in the middle of the sand. I wanted to walk along the water's edge, but my focus was the sand, so I shifted gears and moved to the middle away from the water.

Life is great when we walk with God. It's like nothing else compares to His presence and all the benefits that come with knowing Him. We want to stay there. It's like wanting to walk near the water's edge and not in the sand.

Christians become ineffective for God when we choose to stay in a vacuum, even if it's near Him. Just like I wanted to walk by the cool refreshing water, you may want to stay near God where you find peace, hope, love, you name it. But God calls you out into the world to let others see what you have in Him. He calls you to walk in the sand.

Sometimes the call takes you away from the Water's edge.

"The man ... begged to go with Him, but Jesus sent him away." - Luke 8:38-39

It's Not Right

This one wasn't right either. First it was the wrong shape then it was the wrong size. Now it's the wrong color. Every stone I found to complete my castle wasn't what I was looking for. It just wasn't right. I wanted to give up.

How many of us have times in our lives when we think something should be a certain way … and it isn't? Our life was supposed to be this way, but it's nothing like we imagined—not even close for some of us. It can be disappointing. We may want to throw in the towel. We want to quit.

Things may not always go your way. Your life may be completely different than what you imagined or thought it should be. I found a stone to finish my castle that day, but it was different than what I wanted or imagined it should be. You know what? It worked. God gives us what works even if it's not what we were looking for.

"And my God will meet all your needs according to the riches of His glory in Christ Jesus."
- Philippians 4:19

Deep Waters

I watched as the young dad took his child out into deep waters. The child was scared. I remember those days ... my dad taking me out over my head. He never was afraid but I was.

Haven't we all been afraid of things? Maybe it's losing a job or not making ends meet. Maybe it's facing illness or even death. Maybe it's being alone or unaccepted. Or maybe it's just the unknown. God allows us to face our fears.

My dad was never afraid when he took me out over my head. You have a Father who is not afraid either. Why? He is not over His head. God knows He can handle every situation you face. You don't have to be afraid. The things that scare you don't scare Him. He is taller than the deep waters you find yourself in.

Have a little faith. Your Father is not over His Head.

"Immediately Jesus reached out His hand and caught him. 'You of little faith,' He said, 'Why did you doubt?'" - Matthew 14:31

Biting Flies

I was finishing my walk along the beach when I noticed a man swatting at the flies. The flies were biting, but they didn't seem that bad to me. He was batting at them so much it made me wonder if there was something drawing the flies to him.

Don't we sometimes think we can get away with things? We know the natural consequences, but we think we can ignore them anyway and not have to deal with them. It's like sitting next to something drawing flies and thinking you won't have to swat at them.

The Bible suggests that, if you don't want to get burned, don't play with fire. You can't expect to do things wrong and not get the fallout from it. That's another part of growing up—realizing consequences come with certain actions.

If you don't want to deal with biting flies, don't sit next to them.

"Can a man scoop fire into his lap without his clothes being burned?" - Proverb 6:27

Strong Winds

The higher I went on the boardwalk, the windier it became. When I felt the strong winds blowing, I was a little afraid. My confidence shrunk. My thoughts were telling me I could be blown off or the boardwalk could be blown over.

We set out to accomplish something admirable, but the more we get into it, the more difficult it becomes. We wonder if we can really handle it or if we will get blown away like a strong wind blowing across the boardwalk. Our confidence shrinks from the opposition and we start to question whether what we are doing is really a good idea or not.

I made my way across the whole boardwalk without getting blown off. Something inside kept me going and kept me from blowing away. That something was Jesus. Jesus gives you what you need to overcome and withstand any obstacle you face. He keeps you going.

Jesus is greater than strong, blowing winds.

"The One who is in you is greater than the one who is in the world." - 1 John 4:4

April

"See the Water when you take your eyes off
the sand."

Survival

For some reason, my son and I we were not walking along the water's edge. It turns out that was a good thing or we would have missed it - a tiny little turtle making its way across the sand towards the water. The turtle became our focus as we picked it up and watched what it did. We talked about what turtles ate and about having a pet turtle. Every time we set it down though, it kept heading towards Lake Michigan.

That tiny turtle had one focus—to get to the water. First Corinthians 9:26 tells us to run a race to win the prize. In other words, live life to find God. No matter what distractions and unplanned circumstances we find ourselves in, keep focused. In every situation, turn back to God. For that tiny turtle, it was probably a matter of survival to make it to the water. It is a matter of survival for us too. We need God just as the turtle needed the water.

There was no new pet turtle in our home that day. Instead, we watched as he made it to the water. Will you keep your focus until you make it to the Water?

"Therefore I do not run like someone running aimlessly." – 1 Corinthians 9:26

New Paths

To find an Indian bead in the sand is like finding a needle in a haystack so normally I walk along the edge of the water where there's a better chance of finding them. I felt a nudge to head inland about 10-15 feet and there in my path was not only an Indian bead, but a hard-to-find big Indian bead. Happily, I scooped it up.

God's Spirit leads us into new paths—paths we wouldn't normally take, paths that may seem stupid. We take the logical paths offering the best chance for success.

If I would not have listened to the nudge to change course, I never would have found that Indian bead. And I never would have had my lesson from God teaching me about being led by the Spirit.

God's Spirit nudges you into new paths and, by listening, you find your blessings.

"I will lead by ways they have not known."
- Isaiah 42:16

Eyes on the Sand

With my head bent down and my eyes focused on the sand, I realized I was missing the beauty of the day. I was walking right through it and not seeing the waves roll or the sun shining on the water.

Don't we all get too caught up in life at times? Our focus seems to be on our daily To Do lists. We hurry here and there, taking care of things as if the world will fall apart if we fail to do all on our plate. Just like when I kept my head down focusing on the sand, we go through life focused on all that it brings. It's in those times that we can miss the beautiful things God has for us.

I was lucky enough to realize that before my walk ended. I saw the beautiful sun shining on the water. I heard the talk and laughter of families. I experienced the gentle roll of the waves and then I headed back to my life of busyness and demands.

Get your eyes off the sand. Lift your head up and experience the beauty God has for you.

"But You, Lord, are a shield around me, my glory, the One who lifts my head high." - Psalm 3:3

Stone-less

She was collecting Petoskey stones for her landscape but was not having much luck finding them. I wondered if she would go home stone-less.

Most if not all of us have had days when we don't measure up in our own eyes. We don't recognize our talents and the things we have to offer. We may feel like we are of little value. We may feel like that lady on the beach … stone-less with no value.

People may judge you based on your accomplishments, but in God's eyes your value is not in what you are able to do. He loves His children and He doesn't put a condition on that. He loves you whether you have a lot of abilities or you don't. He made you the way you are, and you are good in His eyes. Nothing can change His love for you, not even the abundance or the lack of talent.

God loves you.

"Not anything … in all creation will be able to separate us from the love of God that is in Christ Jesus our Lord." - Romans 8:39

Peace-full Walks

My walks are a way of clearing my head when life gets crazy. After a walk, I head home feeling a bit more together … a bit more at peace.

Don't we all have days where nothing seems to go right? Our To-Do lists shout with demands. Our best efforts don't even come close. The pains and hurts start crushing in.

It's on those days that I take walks. It's not a walk on Weko Beach that clears my head. It is time focused on God and His Word that brings peace and escape from the hectic scene of life.

Peace can be found anywhere when you look for God. It is found in the middle of harsh circumstances when you have no understanding of what's happening or how to work your way out of it. That is God's peace.

Peace-full walks are found on a walk with God, not on a beach.

"And the peace of God, which transcends all understanding, will guard your hearts and your minds in Christ Jesus." - Philippians 4:7

Scary Heights

I'm not big on heights. I like to keep my two feet on the ground. I feel more in control. Now here I was walking up a steep boardwalk and feeling uncomfortable. The higher I went, the less control I had and the scarier it got.

Taking the high road isn't always easy. It sounds good, but it can be hard. We may be taken out of our comfort zone and put into the unfamiliar. We get scared when that happens. We lose control and become afraid.

Sometimes it's nice to know you are not in control and God is. He made and controls everything. He knows how to deliver you. Don't you think when you try to do something His way—to take the high road—He is happy about it? He promises to deliver you from all your fears, even the steep boardwalks you find yourself on.

You have nothing to fear when you take the High road.

"I sought the Lord, and He answered me; He delivered me from all my fears." – Psalm 34:4

Swim Together

Don't swim alone. That's one of the rules of swimming. There is safety swimming with other people. If there is a problem, someone is there to help.

We think we can handle whatever comes our way. We don't want to rely on others let alone admit we need help. Maybe it's our pride or our ego getting in the way. It's like swimming alone at the beach.

There is safety in numbers. The Bible even talks of this. Others are watching your back while you watch theirs. It's not a bad idea, especially when you don't have eyes on the back of your head. They may know things that could help you out while you know things that could help them out. It's a biblical principle and one that will keep you swimming safely.

Be safe. Swim with others.

"For lack of guidance a nation falls, but victory is won through many advisers."
- Proverb 11:14

Under-rated

I was the only one here. No one wanted to be out in the cold when they could be in a warm, toasty home. I thought to myself, *Boy! Am I lucky! I have my own private beach all to myself today!*

Some of us aren't comfortable being alone. It almost seems like we are judged by how many Facebook friends we have or by the number of invites we receive. We get caught up running in circles impressing people and we become comfortable in that environment. Being at a beach alone can be foreign to us.

Jesus purposely took time for Himself. The Bible tells of a time that He dismissed even His closest disciples in order to be alone. He sent them away. If you find yourself in a time when you are alone, maybe God has dismissed those people so you can get your much-needed alone time with Him. He may just want to connect with you today.

Alone time on the beach is under-rated.

"After He had dismissed them, He went up on a mountainside by Himself to pray."
- Matthew 14:23

Race out of the Water

My siblings and I all wanted the air mattress my parents just finished blowing up. We raced out of the water to the blanket to be the first one to get it. I ran as fast as I could but running against the water isn't easy. It slowed me down.

We don't always want to live life the way God wants us to. If we are honest, we have had times where we knew the right thing to do, but we did the wrong thing anyway. What did it get us? Probably more trouble than it was worth.

Jesus told Saul that it was hard to kick against the goads. In other words, it is hard to go against superior power. Life is harder when you don't obey God. You may not get into any noticeable trouble doing things wrong, but who knows how much you are hindered?

It's easier to walk with God than to run against Him.

"Why are you persecuting Me? It is hard for you to kick against the goads." - Acts 26:14

Small and Lopsided

It's not what I would have chosen. Just like every other day I wanted to find the best perfectly formed Indian bead. This was far from it—small, lopsided. I decided to hang on to it, though, since it was all I found so far.

All of us probably have something we don't like about ourselves, whether it's physical or situational. We want to be like that illusive yet perfectly formed Indian bead. We want to have the perfect body or the perfect life. Life isn't like that though and so we hang onto what we have.

God designed you for His purposes. Just as Indian beads come well-rounded or lopsided, small or big, long or short, you have characteristics and circumstances different from everyone else. It's what you do with your differences that really make the difference.

Hang onto your uniqueness and do something with it.

"But in fact God has placed the parts in the body, every one of them, just as He wanted them to be." - 1 Corinthians 12:18

Stepping into Footprints

The climb ahead was not going to be easy. Climbing Old Baldy never is. As a child, I learned the climb was easier when I stepped into the footprints of beachgoers who climbed the dune before me. It was almost like they paved the way for me a little bit.

Some generations seem to approach life as if they are the first to experience whatever they are going through and yet history repeats itself. As a young teen I remember consciously deciding to listen to the adults in my life even if I didn't necessarily agree with them simply because they had been my age before and may have faced the same situations at some point. It's much like stepping into an earlier beachgoer's footprints while climbing Old Baldy. We let them pave the way making our going a little easier. Wisdom is found among the older generations. Why not use that to your advantage?

Find wisdom in the footprints of those who went before you.

"Is not wisdom found among the aged?"
- Job 12:12

Drive, Walk, Bike

I drive to Weko Beach. Others are within walking distance, and still others ride their bikes. We all get there in different ways.

Don't we sometimes judge others and their relationship with God by the church they go to. We weigh their authenticity based on the church they attend. It's almost like thinking a day at the beach is not as good for people who get there using a different mode of transportation.

If you think about it, there are many different ways people came to Jesus in the Bible. There were the twelve disciples He specifically called; there were the sick He healed; and there were still others who came only after hearing of His life, death, and resurrection. One denomination may help someone grow closer to God than another. Isn't that what really matters?

There are many ways to Jesus, but only One Way to the Father.

"I am the way and the truth and the life. No one comes to the Father except through Me."
- John 14:6

Rolled Away

I came back and, to my dismay, the stones I pushed into the castle wall had fallen out. They were supposed to be windows. As I stood there, another one rolled off and on to the sand. I wasn't too happy about it.

There was a stone that rolled away a long time ago. It didn't make everyone happy but, for others, it made all the difference in the world. It changed the lives of those who saw it and believed. It gave them hope in difficult times and showed them how to love others, including the unlovable. It opened the door to valuable advice and counsel. It became a refuge from cruel circumstances and provided strength against things bigger than themselves. That stone rolled just once and left the door open to the empty grave of Jesus.

Thank You, God, for this one stone that rolled away.

"They found the stone rolled away from the tomb." - Luke 24:2

The Empty Tower

If you walk south along Weko Beach, you will pass an empty old brick tower. I often wonder about it but I never have the guts to go investigate. What was it used for? Why is it empty?

Every day there is news of violence and terror, of Christian persecutions, promotions of beliefs contrary to the Word, and of outright sin. It is enough to make us cower in a corner.

The Tower of Babel shows the unlimited, out-of-the-box ability God has. When the people decided to build a tower to form a one-world nation where everyone lived together and where they could make a name for themselves, God had a different plan. He confused their language and the people deserted the tower they were building.

You don't have to be afraid of the world and all that's wrong. If God can change the world's language just like that, He can handle what is going on today. He has more power than all the nations put together. Empty towers remind us God has the final word.

"Great is the Lord in Zion; He is exalted over all the nations." - Psalm 99:22

Slivers

Running my hand across the railing was not a good idea. A small sliver of wood stuck in my finger and it didn't feel good. Slivers happen even on boardwalks.

Sometimes our calling in life can make us feel like we are immune to problems. Things can feel so good we can't imagine what kind of harm or difficulty can touch us. We may even get a big head, thinking others will have these problems but we are untouchable because we are doing what we have been called to do.

Don't make the mistake of thinking someone isn't following their calling because of the problems they have. Everyone gets slivers. So what do you do? It would be hard to take out someone's sliver when you are dealing with your own.

Take your sliver out before taking out another's.

"First take the plank out of your own eye."
- Matthew 7:5

Good Seats

They start gathering around on the boardwalk in the evenings, probably trying to get a good place on one of the benches. These old-timers enjoy talking with each other as they wait for the sun to go down. It may not be the same people every time, but they look happy and content just being there.

We look forward to things in our lives, whether it's a once-in-a-lifetime event or a simple every day activity. I look forward to my walks on Weko Beach just as the old-timers look forward to sitting on a bench enjoying the sunset and talking with others.

What do you look forward to? The Bible talks of the days when Jesus will live among us and rule over us in righteousness and justice. There won't be any wrongs done to you. Everything will be fair. Old-timers will sit in the streets. They won't be too sick to do so. It's not that way now, but some days I think Weko Beach is about as close as it will get!

Look forward to good seats on the streets of Jerusalem!

"Once again men and women of ripe old age will sit in the streets of Jerusalem." - Zechariah 8:4

Winter Walks

Lake Michigan had frozen for the winter and snow covered everything. On days like this, I hesitate. During my winter walks, I can't always tell where the beach ends and the water begins. The line between the two becomes indistinguishable.

Many of us like to compartmentalize things. What we do in one place is separate from what we do in another. We may do the same thing with God. He is Lord of our life in one area but not in others. We compartmentalize Him.

If you really are serious about God being Lord of your life, take the walls down. De-compartmentalize Him. Make Him Lord of all your life—not just on Sunday mornings, not just around other church people, not just when you are around others, and not just when you can't get away with something. Let His influence in your life become so de-compartmentalized that people can't tell where it starts and where it ends—like a winter walk on the beach. You can't tell where the water begins and ends. A de-compartmentalized walk can distinguish God more.

"I am the Alpha and the Omega, the First and the Last, the Beginning and the End."
- Revelations 22:13

Changing Course

There is a stream running from the campground at Weko Beach into Lake Michigan. One day as I was walking, I met a guy with a shovel. It stirred my interest, so I asked what it was for. He told me he and his family would come down to Weko Beach and change the course of the stream.

We have our goals, things we want out of life. We plot and plan in the hopes of accomplishing them. We put our shovels to the sand in an effort to change the course of our lives. Our effort is not a bad thing, but God is the changing force behind every goal. He is the One directing the course.

Just as the man I met shoveled to change the course of the stream, you too can make efforts to change the course of your life. Just as the water ultimately was the power behind the change of the stream's course, God is the power behind your life and the change of course it can take. Shovel when you can, but let the Water work its wonders.

"I am making a way in the wilderness and streams in the wasteland." - Isaiah 43:19

Star Indian Beads

Have you ever looked closely at Indian beads? I assumed they all had circular centers. It wasn't until I really look at one that I noticed it had a star in the center. I got into my jar of Indian beads and noticed others with a star too. Next time you run across an Indian bead check it out. See if it has a star.

There are many, many blessings to be thankful about each day, but there is one blessing outshining the rest. That one blessing is Jesus and a personal relationship with Him. He blesses us in many ways and sometimes we miss seeing Him in them. It's like finding an Indian bead with a star and missing the star.

Next time you experience a blessing, take the time to really look at it. Do you see the Star in the middle of it all?

Blessings become personal when you see Him in it.

"Where is the One who has been born King of the Jews? We saw His star when it rose and have come to worship Him." - Matthew 2:2

Safe Play

I watched the young kids as they played. They played without a care in the world, unaware of the potential dangers around them.

We set rules for our kids. Don't swim too far out. Swim with others. Stay where I can see you. These are some common rules parents set for their kids at the beach. We set still other rules for them when we aren't at the beach. Rules like "Let me know where you are going and text me when you get there" or Don't play in the street." The rules are there for their safety.

You may always have the safety and well-being of your children on your mind, but there will be a day when parents will not have to worry about that. Your kids will be able to swim out as far as they want. They will be able to play in the streets. For now, you do what you can for their well-being until the day comes that the Bible talks about.

"The city streets will be filled with boys and girls playing there." - Zechariah 8:5

Perfect Sand Crab

I played with the sand as my kids swam. Their toys reminded me of my childhood. I picked up a mold and, with wet sand, I created the perfect image of a sand crab. If I had tried to make it without the mold, it would fall far short of what it was meant to be.

God decided to create us in His image. Since that day though, we have sinned, and our perfect image of God has fallen short. We are like a sand crab built without a mold.

But God gave you His Word. It molds and shapes your life. It molds and shapes your attitudes and character. God also gave you a perfect example—Jesus—to look at as you try to live. You will fall short but fill your heart and mind with His Word. It's like putting wet sand into the mold God created. One day the creation will come out in the perfect image God created you to be—in His image.

Fill your heart and mind with God's word to become like Him.

"Let Us make mankind in Our image."
- Genesis 1:26

Something New

The focus of most of my walks along Weko Beach is collecting Indian beads and learning what God would teach me in the process. I've learned a lot during those walks. I learned about blessings through Indian beads, and I wanted to be blessed so, naturally, that was my focus. This day was different. My focus changed.

Don't we sometimes miss things because we are so focused on something else? We want it so badly that we can see nothing else. We miss things right under our nose, not realizing the value it offers us. That day on the beach, I was so busy looking for an Indian bead that I missed the stones. It's like that ... we get so focused on getting the blessing sometimes that we miss the God-given talent He gave to us to acquire the blessing. The point is ... our talents are blessings. God gave me a new lesson. He taught me that abilities are blessings too.

Stones may be the channel for your blessing.

"See, I am doing a new thing. Do you not perceive it?" - Isaiah 43:19

The Tree

There is a broken tree sitting off in the distant dune as you walk south of Weko Beach. It is a tall tree stump with no branches or leaves. It reminds me of the song "The Old Rugged Cross" written by George Bennard.

It can be hard to see Jesus in our everyday lives. If it isn't the busyness keeping us from Him, it is our human nature looking at what we want to see.

The first day I noticed the tree standing alone, high on top of the dune, "The Old Rugged Cross" was playing in my head. It reminded me of what Jesus did for me in the middle of my busyness. Here on Weko Beach sits a tree reminding me of something so long ago and so far away.

When an encouraging and comforting word is needed, when a reminder of Jesus would be welcomed, look around you. Listen. The Holy Spirit is at work putting a song in your head and a tree on a hill.

"The Holy Spirit … will teach you all things and will remind you of everything I have said to you."
- John 14:26

Side Paths

While walking on the boardwalk, I was surprised to see the sandy side paths leading away from it. At any point I could climb over the rail and take a different path.

It's so easy to get distracted. We set a goal. We aim for the high road and, along the way, something distracts us like a sandy side path offering an enticing change of scenery. Before we know it, we have given up on our goals. We have given up on our high road and we find ourselves somewhere we never aimed to be. Life has a way of doing that.

How do you stay on target living a life for God? How do you stay on the boardwalk? The Bible tells us to love God more than the world. Decide today that God is most important to you. When distractions show up along the path, you already know what is most important, and every decision you make should support that.

Love God most. That is what keeps you on the boardwalk.

"Do not love the world or anything in the world."
- 1 John 2:15

Am I Getting a Tan?

I rolled over on my blanket and pulled at my strap. "Am I getting a tan?" It was a familiar question my sister and our friends would ask each other as we laid on the beach in the sun.

"You are what you eat." Our parents and teachers taught this as a way to get us to eat healthy. We could take it a step further: "You are what you watch on TV." "You are what you think." It's the whole idea of making choices to get the results you want. Like spending time at the beach … the more time we spend under the sun, the more likely we will tan.

It's the same in your relationship with God. The more time you spend in His Word and actively pursuing Him, the more you learn about Him. You begin to take on His characteristics. You start to think like Him. You like the things He likes and hate the things He hates. When you tan in the "Son," you begin to take on His image.

"For those God foreknew He also predestined to be conformed to the image of His Son, that He might be the firstborn among many brothers and sisters." – Romans 8:29

Cross Over the Log

I never know if I will be walking south of the creek on Weko Beach in the winter. In the warm months I wade through it, but in the cold months it's way too cold. I don't want to take off my shoes and wade through it then.

There are times we don't know what to do. We come up against something and we don't have the answers. What we have done in the past won't work today. We can no longer wade through the creek as we have before.

One of the benefits of a relationship with God is He shows you how to handle things. When you come up against something new or different, He provides the way. It never fails on my walks during the colder seasons. A log has been laid across the creek connecting the two sides. I easily cross over the log. When what has worked before no longer works, God may have already provided another way.

Look for a log and cross over.

"I will instruct you and teach you in the way you should go." – Psalm 32:8

Unknown Waters

Things were a mess. I had no idea what to do and I felt totally at a loss. I was thrown one of life's curve balls, and my future was very unclear. I stood looking out across Lake Michigan, wondering. The waters were vast and unending. I had no idea what laid beneath just as I had no idea what my future held.

We can never really know all that God has planned for us. His ways are immeasurable and unseen. Impossibilities are possible because of His unlimited resources and power. I learned an important lesson as I stood there wondering. I could settle for a future I didn't want based on circumstances I knew and could see at the time. Or, I could hang in there waiting for a future I'd rather have and one I couldn't see, faithfully relying on and hoping in God and His plans for me. I gave God a chance and found my future again.

Sometimes you need to do nothing so God can do something.

"What no eye has seen, what no ear has heard, and what no human mind has conceived, the things God has prepared for those who love Him." – 1 Corinthians 2:9

The Priceless Bead

I found the Indian bead of all Indian beads—the one I had hoped to find. It was priceless in my eyes. All those days of hoping and walking along Weko Beach finally became real.

Finding Jesus through all the chaos of other "blessings" is a precious thing. The Bible tells of a merchant looking for that perfect pearl and, when he found it, he sold all he had to buy it.

I have taken many walks along Weko Beach looking for that perfect, priceless Indian bead. I felt blessed by the Indian beads I picked up along the way as they taught me lessons about God and life. But I found it was not so much the Indian beads (or even the priceless Indian bead) that blessed me as much as my walk with God guiding me, reassuring me, encouraging me, and loving me. My walks with God became the priceless, perfect blessing I needed and searched for. All I had to do was take the time to walk on Lake Michigan. Will you walk with God and find your priceless blessing?

"When he had found one of great value, he went away and sold everything he had and bought it." - Matthew 13:46

A Good Book

I passed by a man sitting along Lake Michigan in a beach chair reading a book. I've done that myself—taken a book out to the beach to read. It's a great way to unwind.

We stress over many things. Demands pile up adding to our never-ending to-do lists. The farther behind we get, the more we stress out and the more worked up we become. Our lives seem out of balance and it feels like we are tottering on the brink of the next calamity.

A balanced life doesn't have to be illusive. It may take hard choices and constant monitoring, but it could well be worth it. Do you want a balanced life? Time in God's Word gives you the right perspective when prioritizing. It gives wisdom and the strength to say "No" to demands setting you free from them. The biggest priority is staying in the Word. It lights the way, setting all other priorities for you.

There's nothing like the Good Book on a day at the beach!

"The unfolding of Your Word gives light; it gives understanding to the simple." - Psalm 119:130

A Line in the Sand

Someone drew a line in the wet sand. I wondered why. Was it drawn as a dare for someone to cross or as a boundary setting the limits to how far someone would go?

We all reach some pivotal points in our lives where we face decisions affecting our future and maybe even the future of others around us. It's in those times that we are put to the test. A line is drawn and we decide what we will and will not do. Committing ourselves to Jesus is one of those pivotal points.

You are either for Him or against Him. When you are for Jesus, you draw the line refusing to do things against His Word. You draw the line refusing wrong opportunities that come. You draw the line even when those wrong opportunities benefit you. Drawing the line means something to you and affects both you and those around you.

Where will you draw the line?

"Whoever is not with Me is against Me."
- Matthew 12:30

May

"Indian beads come from the Water."

Out of Reach

The water was too cold for me, so I walked in the dry sand not wanting to get wet. I didn't roll up my jeans and I left my shoes on. Then it hit—that one wave reaching farther than I thought it could. My jeans and my shoes were soaked.

Aren't there times in our lives when we feel like we are out of God's reach? Maybe it's because our problems seem too big or maybe we feel like God can't love us enough to care about us. Sometimes we may even want it that way so we can handle life on our own. I didn't want to get wet that day on Weko Beach, but it reminded me that we are never out of God's reach even if we want to be.

God reassures you that He will never leave you. He will be with you throughout your life. He reminds you of His unconditional and constant love for you. You are not alone and you are not on your own. You are always within God's reach.

"For I am with you; do not be dismayed, for I am your God. I will strengthen you and help you."
- Isaiah 41:10

Washed Up

An Indian bead was floating back and forth with each wave. Those are the hard ones to grab. I'd have to be quick about it before the waves washed it away for good.

It's so easy to miss our blessings and to take things for granted. We focus on the wrong and miss everything else. Even if we recognize a blessing, we may not recognize the source. Just as Lake Michigan washes up an Indian bead and delivers it to the beach, God is the Giver of our blessings. All you have to do is open your eyes and recognize where they come from. The Source is not from your circumstances. It's not from your abilities or from someone else. The Source may deliver your blessings through those things, but they are not the Source.

Indian beads are washed up onto the shore through the water by the hand of God.

"Every good gift and every perfect gift is from above." - James 1:17

Brush It Off

I can still hear my mom telling me to get all the sand off my feet when we were packing up to go home. I told my kids the same thing. "Brush the sand off your feet. I don't want it in my car or dragged into the house."

Don't we all have times when others don't accept us? Maybe they mistreat us. It becomes baggage we carry around. Jesus sent His disciples to go out and preach, but before they left He instructed them to wipe off their feet if people didn't accept them.

I always thought it was a strange thing for Jesus to say until I understood it. In other words, brush it off and leave it in God's hands. It's like getting all the sand off and leaving it at the beach.

Brush it off and leave it in God's hands.

"If anyone will not welcome you or listen to your words, leave that home or town and shake off the dust from your feet." - Matthew 10:14

Walk the Walk

I'm not walking Weko Beach when I am working around the house. I'm not walking Weko Beach when I am walking in the neighborhood. I'm not walking Weko Beach when I'm sitting on a bench on the boardwalk.

We can fool ourselves into thinking we are living the way God wants us to. We brush off those little offenses and refuse to acknowledge our role in problems with others. We think we are in the clear when no one else is around to see. It's like thinking we are walking on Weko Beach when we really are doing something else.

Jesus sees and knows how you live your life. Take some time to evaluate yourself, your actions, and your life. Are you walking the walk? Are you living life as Jesus did? If not, why not and how could you change? Just saying you are doesn't mean you are. You have to live it out.

A walk on the beach is not a walk on the beach unless you are walking on the beach.

"Whoever claims to live in Him must live as Jesus did." - 1 John 2:6

The Farthest

Who could toss their stone the farthest out into the lake? It was a game of competition and usually the strongest or most athletic person would win.

We get down on ourselves when we can't deliver like the next person. We want to throw our stone out as far as possible—to throw it out the farthest as if all God sees is how far we can throw our stones.

God knows your abilities. He knows how far your abilities will go. It's no surprise to Him when you can't deliver as well as the next person. Why? When you can't, God can. So when you get disappointed with yourself and when you are kicking yourself for not having the ability you think you should have, remember this:

God cares more about your heart than how far you toss your stones.

"Each of you should give what you have decided in your heart to give … for God loves a cheerful giver." - 2 Corinthians 9:7

A Corn Cob

I now include a list of odd things I see along Weko Beach. These are things out-of-place, things you wouldn't expect to see on a beach. The corn cob was one. I would expect to see it on a farm before seeing it here.

Haven't we all had times when we wanted to do something but it seemed like the wrong time and the wrong place? It's like a good opportunity presenting itself in the wrong environment—such as a corn cob on a beach instead of a farm.

It was a Sunday. The disciples were hungry and walking in the middle of a corn field. What better opportunity to fulfill their hunger than to pick some corn and eat it? The Pharisees came down hard on them for grabbing the opportunity at the wrong time. Sometimes Jesus presents opportunities at inopportune times and places, but ...

Go with it and pick the corn.

"Look! Your disciples are doing what is unlawful on the Sabbath." - Matthew 12:2

Checkpoints

There are posts every so often along the boardwalk. These posts are planted deep into the sand and are part of the foundational structure holding it up. They are like checkpoints connecting the boardwalk to the foundation so that all remains well along the way.

When we set out on our calling, all seems right and in place. Our faith, our confidence, our attitudes, our hearts are lined up and right where they need to be. Along the way, though, we can get out of alignment. It can slow down or even stop what we were called to do. We need checkpoints along the way.

Unbiased, self-evaluations are a great way to stay on track. Being open and honest with yourself is like a boardwalk checkpoint along the way. You stop and honestly evaluate yourself in the light of God's Word.

Stop at a checkpoint.

"I have considered my ways and have turned my steps to Your Statutes." – Psalm 119:59

Progress

He sat in the sand near the water's edge not quite ready to go in. As he grew older, my son headed out a little farther. I would watch and set limits as to how far my kids could venture out until they were old enough to decide for themselves.

It's not always easy to set limits for our kids. We do though because we have their best interests in mind. We set limits to keep them from wrong or from harm. Even too much of a good thing requires limits. We monitor their progress and allow them to go deeper as they grow older.

Progressing in your faith and in your walk with Jesus eventually becomes a responsibility you grow into just like children growing into adulthood deciding for themselves how far to go out into the water. You start out with the simple things like "Jesus loves me this I know" and grow until you read your Bible on your own without being told. Then you study and learn and apply it to your daily life.

How are you progressing? Are you growing in your walk with Jesus?

"I gave you milk, not solid food, for you were not yet ready for it." – 1 Corinthians 3:2

Layers

Summer had come to an end and the weather was beginning to change. The air was brisk, so I was thankful for the added layers I had put on.

We prepare for many things throughout our lives. Maybe it's an exam at school or team tryouts. Maybe it's wedding plans or the birth of a child. We even prepare for the unexpected … we buy health insurance, life insurance, and auto insurance.

How do you prepare for unexpected troubles? You will have them—the Bible says so. Why not prepare for them? It's like putting extra layers on for a walk on the beach in cold weather. Read and meditate on God's Word. It builds strong faith able to stand in troubled times.

Dressing in layers gives added protection from the cold.

"Put on the full armor of God, so that you can take your stand against the devil's schemes." – Ephesians 6:11

Reflections

The sun was setting, leaving its reflection on the water. Myself, along with all the other beachgoers, looked out over Weko Beach as the sun went down. It made me think about reflections on the water.

In our reflections, we see ourselves but not always clearly. Maybe there's a ripple of water distorting our view. Life can have a rippling effect on the way we see ourselves. It can distort what we see and we forget who God made us to be. When we look at ourselves through His eyes, we see ourselves the way He does.

Something else ... God sees you looking at Him. Just like a reflection on the water, He is looking right back at you. That's a comforting thought. When you go through difficult times, when people mistreat you, when you are forgotten, and when you seem to be unvalued, God sees. You can find comfort knowing He knows when you are looking for Him, and it pleases Him.

"The eyes of the Lord are everywhere, keeping watch on the wicked and the good."
– Proverb 15:3

A Keeper

I put the time and effort in and found what I came for. With Indian bead in hand, I continued on.

When we want something, we put forth the time and effort to get it. We work day after day towards that goal. Finally, the day comes when we find what we went after. What do we do? We hang onto it. We don't throw it away after all we have put into it.

The point is this: Jesus is valuable. He is worth the time and effort. He is worth searching for day after day and, when you find Him, why would you throw that out? Just as I searched and found that Indian bead along Weko Beach and did not throw it back, search for Jesus and hang on to Him. Your own personal relationship with Him is worth the effort to find and to keep.

What will you do with Jesus? Will He be a keeper?

"Do not give dogs what is sacred; do not throw your pearls to pigs." – Matthew 7:6

Light on Your Feet

Some kids are content to sit in the sand and play. They have no interest in going into the water. Others—you can't keep them out. Their every move leaves you light on your feet, ready to jump in.

We are ready as parents to do what we need to do to help our kids. It can be hard and confusing at times. Parents don't have all the answers, and we don't always know what to do.

Our children don't usually realize their need for us to have all the answers or to faithfully care for them. You may be the very light and the faithful care God has graced their lives with. It's a daunting task—one you may struggle with. But He does have the answers and He is faithful to guide you as you guide them. Help them to know Jesus.

Be light on your feet, ready to jump in. God will be your light and faithful care.

"Send me Your light and Your faithful care, let them lead me; let them bring me to Your holy mountain, to the place where You dwell."
– Psalm 43:3

New Sand Sculptures

As a kid spending time at the beach, I learned pretty fast that it was easier to build things with wet sand. Wet sand packs better and holds better. Creations take shape with it. They no longer look like dry heaps of sand piled into nothingness.

Life has a way of wearing us out and making us feel like we are nothing. We see other people's accomplishments and, while we may be happy for them, inside we stand criticized and condemned for not accomplishing our own goals. We see the beauty of other people's lives but only see the scars and flaws of our own. It's internal self-condemnation we quietly carry—an ugly, old pile of sand amounting to nothing.

When you have a personal relationship with Christ, you become a new creation. It's like adding water to the sand. It takes on a new form—a new creation. You no longer have to condemn yourself. Christ will help you overcome your self-condemnations and make you into what you were meant to be. Add some Water to the mix and come up with something new.

"Therefore, if anyone is in Christ, the new creation has come." – 2 Corinthians 5:17

Stop the Erosion

The erosion of Weko Beach was very apparent this summer. The sandy beach was disappearing. The large stone boulders extended out into Lake Michigan, set there to prevent further erosion. Their purpose on the beach was clear.

We have talents yet we may not always be sure how to use them. We wonder what they're good for. We can't always see how our talents are good for anything.

Just like the big stone boulders extending out into Lake Michigan to prevent erosion, you can use your talents in the same way. God asks who will go. You can use your talents to stand against the wrong so prevalent in this world. God sets you here, at this time, and with your specific abilities to stand against all that's wrong around you.

Want to stop the erosion? "Here am I. Send me."

"Then I heard the voice of the Lord saying, 'Whom shall I send? And who will go for us?' And I said, 'Here am I. Send me.'" – Isaiah 6:8

The Painted Mural

The concrete filtration structure on Weko Beach has a mural painted around the bottom portion. I know this because a few years back, the waters of Lake Michigan did not surround the structure. People could actually walk around it and see the whole thing. Today, I look at it and wonder. I can still see the mural on this side of the structure, but I wonder if the paint has held up under the battering waves on the other side.

"Don't judge a book by its cover" yet many times we still judge situations and people by what we see. It's like looking at the concrete filtration structure on Weko Beach and judging it by the mural we see painted on the one side without seeing the other side.

It's easy to pass judgement on what you can see. It's hard to hold your judgement when you can't see the whole picture. Real growth and maturity is when you hold your mouth and your opinions, realizing you may not see everything. God sees the whole mural.

"People look at the outward appearance, but the Lord looks at the heart." – 1 Samuel 16:7

Nothing More

I just wanted to walk along the beach. Nothing more. I didn't want to search for Indian beads. I didn't want to get anything more out of this than to just walk along the water's edge and listen to the sound of the waves.

Don't we often get caught up going to God for what we can get out of Him? Who better to go to, but our need and our desire for God should go beyond that.

Do you sometimes get tired of going to God for the sole purpose of meeting your needs? Do you have moments where you just want to be in His presence and enjoy it without any expectations, like taking a walk on the beach simply to hear and be near the water?

Nothing more but to simply hear and be near the Water—that's joy at its best.

"You will make known to me the path of life; You will fill me with joy in Your presence, with eternal pleasures at Your right hand." – Psalm 16:11

Weathered

One thing I don't like about wooden structures is the newness wears out. It looks old. The boardwalks at Weko Beach are no different. They are made with lumber and look old, weathered, and worn. Sort of reminds me of aging.

Aging doesn't seem to bother us too much when life is new. We have our whole lives ahead of us. We are the new "in" generation. The world places its hope in us, the next generation. But we wake up one day and we are older. We have aged along with our goals. We start assessing what we have accomplished. Did we meet our goals, or did we fall short? We feel worn and tired, struggling from demands placed on us throughout the years.

God promises He is there for you even when you are old and worn, when you feel weathered just like an old piece of treated lumber nailed into place on the boardwalk. He values and cares for you at every stage because He made you.

"Even to your old age and gray hairs I ... will sustain you. I have made you and I will carry you."–Isaiah 46:4

Bare Trees

I always wondered about the trees setting farther back from the water. I never walk through them. Most people don't, and I never want to. During the fall, the brown leaves make them look dark and formidable. I can only imagine the hidden dangers lurking within.

Problems can seem scary—dark and formidable. None of us want to have them. We see potential problems, and we imagine the worse, like looking at the dark trees of Weko Beach and imagining the hidden dangers.

I walked past those trees later, and the leaves were all down. The trees stood exposed and they weren't so scary after all. It's like God blew the brown leaves off the trees letting me see deeper into the woods. God can do that. He can give greater understanding and insight into your unknown scary problems.

Look into the woods with God.

"For the Lord will give you insight into all this."
– 2 Timothy 2:7

Take a Breather

I almost didn't make the trip to Weko Beach. There was so much on my plate—so many demands, things to be done. My feelings were a mix of relief stepping away from it all and also of guilt for being there with so much to do.

We often feel the pressure of demands and cave in. We push off things that really are important. We struggle when we give into the demands, and we struggle when we put the important things first.

The Bible tells us not to wear ourselves out trying to get rich. Maybe it's not just rich in terms of money. Maybe it could also mean rich in terms of acceptance, perfection, image. Many things can distract you, and they may be important, but nothing is more important than your time with God.

Take a breather. Walk near the Water. It's important.

"Do not wear yourself out to get rich."
— Proverb 23:4

A Storm on the Way

No doubt a storm was on the way. The sky was overcast and things looked dismal. Everything seemed bleak. The waves crashed relentlessly on the beach. They had somehow turned from their peaceful, serene state to a powerful force of nature.

When circumstances take a turn for the worse, we look at them and all we see is the bleakness. Nothing seems to be bright with hope. The future can look so dismal in troubling times.

Have you ever noticed how bodies of water change during a storm? Waves appear and become much more powerful. When you face the storms in your life, God's unmatchable power stirs up. He rises up to the occasion just like the waves of Lake Michigan rising up during a storm. When the disciples faced a storm, Jesus rose up and calmed things down. Even the storm was no match for Him.

The power of God rises up with authority over the storms in your life.

"What kind of man is this? Even the wind and the waves obey Him!" – Matthew 8:27

Unstoppable

I wasn't feeling all that great and questioned whether I should even be here. I wanted to walk along the beach, but maybe it wasn't such a good idea. I considered turning back even before starting. Committing to my walk, though, I moved along holding onto the confidence that I could walk the walk.

The Israelites were well known for their backsliding. We are no different. We all have times in our lives when we feel inept and unable to handle what lies ahead of us. It would be easier to turn back—to slide back into the familiar and the comfortable where we know what to do.

I continued on my walk regardless of my lack of confidence and not only did I finish walking, I came out of it with more Indian beads. When you put your confidence in God and what He can do through you, you can accomplish what you set out to do and be blessed in the process.

You are unstoppable when you walk with confidence in God.

"For the Lord will be at your side."
– Proverb 3:26

Sandy Blankets

I was irritated to say the least. *People.* I understand not wanting to take a blanket full of sand home, but why did they have to shake it out right here, sending sand all over me? What were they thinking (or not thinking)?

We have all been hurt by others. We can't escape it. It's part of life. We don't like it. Why, we ask ourselves, did they have to do that? Don't they realize how their actions affect us? It's like someone making a bad choice and shaking the sand from their beach blanket out on us. It stings and it's not fun.

You can't always control what others do. It can harm you, but God calls you to a higher ground. He calls you to love others by living a life considering what you do and how it affects those around you. That is living love out.

Think about it. Where and how will you shake out your sandy blanket?

"Love does no harm to a neighbor. Therefore love is the fulfillment of the law."
— Romans 13:10

Live Life

Not everyone likes to go to the beach. They feel out of place or they don't want to be seen in a bathing suit. They are self-conscious about their bodies.

People don't go to church for different reasons too. They may feel out of place or self-conscious, much like people who avoid going to the beach. They stop attending church and working at their relationship with God.

I learned an important lesson growing up, and it has defined my commitment to God: Don't give up on Him because of how others make you feel. I felt out of place and self-conscious growing up in a broken family, attending a parochial school at a time when divorce was not so common, but God was still God. He led me to not give up on Him because of others or because of how I felt.

Live life. Don't give up the Beach.

"Man shall not live on bread alone, but on every word that comes from the mouth of God."
– Matthew 4:4

Immersed

I lost sight of it. The stone I tossed out into Lake Michigan disappeared. It became immersed in the water.

Don't we hesitate sometimes to commit totally to God? We may do the bare minimum just to get by. We do the right thing when we should be doing a lot more. Our apprehensions cause us to hesitate and only touch the surface of what we can do. Unlike the stone I tossed into Lake Michigan, we don't immerse ourselves.

God wants you to serve Him with a whole heart. That's immersing yourself in His plans. You do that when you commit your talents to whatever He leads you to do and you do it with all you got. It may feel like you lose sight of what you are doing, but that's all part of God's plan, trusting Him when you can't see the outcome.

Toss your stone out into the water and become immersed.

"And serve Him with wholehearted devotion."
- 1 Chronicles 28:9

The Measuring Cup

Of all things—a measuring cup. I suppose someone could have brought it out to the beach to measure food. Or maybe it was used as a toy for the kids to measure sand.

It's not always easy to share. We think in terms of ownership. It's all mine. We want to keep what we can as if we are further ahead by doing so. I struggle sometimes in this area. It's alright if what I have goes to where I think it should go, but heaven forbid, if it goes elsewhere. Heaven forbid, if someone gets more than their share of what I am in control of.

God has something to say about that. It's not just being fair with what you give; it's about trying to stuff as much sand as you can into that measuring cup, filling it full to the brim. And what's in it for you ... a good measure? Pressed down? Overflowing?

"Give, and it will be given to you. A good measure, pressed down, shaken together and running over, will be poured into your lap. For with the measure you use, it will be measured to you." – Luke 6:38

Nailed Down

I noticed all the nails holding the boards in place on the boardwalk. You can't make a structure like this without having something to hold it in place.

Even our loftiest goals need substance to make it a reality. Our ability and our knowledge play a role in meeting them, but our goals are established by doing things right, by doing things God's way.

You can have all the knowledge and ability in the world, but it doesn't mean a thing when you don't do the right thing. When you want to succeed, do what's right. Just as nails are used to hold the boards in place on a boardwalk, righteousness holds you and your calling in place, keeping you on the right track, not swayed with each gust of wind blowing your way.

You hit the nail on the head when you do things right.

"Surely the righteous will never be shaken; they will be remembered forever." – Psalm 112:6

Changing Seasons

Walks along Weko Beach change with the seasons. In the spring, crisp, clean air fills your lungs and sometimes rain clouds loom overhead. Summers are filled with hot sun and the smell of suntan oil. Falls display the golden grasses and cooler air. Winters freeze the lake into place and snow drifts form along the sand.

Changes will come. We may not always know when, but they will come. Sometimes it can be a welcomed change while other times it can be a reluctant change. Life changes for us just as the seasons change on Weko Beach.

You may find security from things that don't change. You can depend on those things, or so you think, until it changes. God never changes. He really is the only dependable thing you have in this life. Bad situations can change to good and good situations can change to bad, but the one constant through either of them is God. He is always there offering strength and guidance through difficult times. And He is always there enjoying the good times with you.

"I the Lord do not change." – Malachi 3:6

One-on-One

For his own reasons, my husband is one of those people who doesn't like to go to the beach. So instead of missing out, I go alone. It bothered me when I saw couples and families and friends there. Here I was alone.

It's not always easy to see the silver lining in situations we find ourselves in. Others seem to have so much more than we have. It's easy to get jealous, feeling like we ended up with the short end of the stick. I felt that way for a long time walking alone on Weko Beach until …

I realized something about my walks. I was connecting with God. I was learning about life, being encouraged in difficult times and able to sort out situations. Over the years, my walks have brought me closer to Him, giving me His understanding and insight into my life. I would have missed out on all that had I shared my walks with anyone else. God changed my lonely walks into special One-on-one times with Him. He can do the same for you.

"And we know that in all things God works for the good of those who love Him, who have been called according to His purpose."
– Romans 8:28

Listening through the Noise

Every other Sunday during the summers, Weko Beach hosts a concert. The band of choice will set up on the deck of the Beach Town Grill, play music, and sing to the crowd sitting below in the sand. On those days, the beach is crowded with people. There is a lot of hub-bub going on and the music can be a distraction from my focus on God. I walk along the water and can hear the small, gentle waves rolling on the beach. The farther away from the concert, the sound of the gentle waves becomes clearer.

Elijah found himself in the mountains waiting to see and hear from God. God wasn't found in the strong winds, the earthquake, or the fire. He was found in a still small voice.

Life offers a lot of obvious avenues to find God, but God comes through quietness and meditation. His still small voice speaks today like the soft gentle wave rolling on the beach.

God quietly speaks as life's concerts continue to play on.

"The Lord was not in the fire. And after the fire came a gentle whisper." – 1 Kings 19:12

Going to the Source

I started thinking ... since Indian beads are actually dead fish bones, and fish live in water, why am I looking for Indian beads in the sand? Why would I not look for them in Lake Michigan? It's too hard to find and grab them while they are in the water. The fact remains, though, that the water is actually the source.

God is the source of our blessings. We may go directly to Him asking for a blessing and become disappointed when we don't get it. Why does that happen? Why aren't we rewarded for going directly to the source of all blessings? Isn't that a good thing?

There's an incident in the New Testament about a born-again sorcerer who approached the disciples to get the power of the Holy Spirit and was reprimanded. Maybe one reason we don't get what we want when we go to God is that He wants to be more than a way to be blessed.

God wants a right heart.

"Because your heart is not right before God..."
- Acts 8:21

Endless Sand

The sand kept going and going. It was endless. It went as far as my eyes could see and beyond. I could see it under the water and it still went beyond that. No matter if I looked up or down Weko Beach, I couldn't see the end of it.

We all want life. We want a good long life—a life without limits much like the sand on any beach. It seems impossible to find it. It's easy to accept that it is impossible, but we don't have to.

God's gift to you is life. That gift is about the here and now … and the hereafter. His gift offers a good life and a long life. The good gift He offers is a life with His never-abandoning presence, a life led by His infinite wisdom, and a life of being loved. The long gift He offers is eternal life. That's a pretty long life!

Grab hold of the good and long life God offers through Jesus.

"But the gift of God is eternal life in Christ Jesus our Lord." – Romans 6:23

June

"Walk on a cloudy day."

A Bucket of Water

The kids were enjoying a little mischief—threatening to throw a bucket of water on their parents. I remember those days when I was threatened with a bucket of cold Lake Michigan. I dreaded the cold water. I wanted to be left alone in my dry skin, even though some cold water would be perfect on a hot summer day.

People don't always like to hear about your faith in God. They want to be left alone with what they are comfortable with.

Sometimes we need to hear about God. We need to hear what He has done for others—the relief He provides in the heat of difficult circumstances. We need to know God is ready and willing to provide something we may not even know is needed.

We all need a good soaking in God even if it comes in the form of an unwanted bucket of water.

"The man went away and told all over town how much Jesus had done for him." – Luke 8:39

Water Over Beads Any Day

I found myself once again at Weko Beach with the goal to experience as much of it as possible before the cold weather kicked in. By the end of my walk, I had a small handful of Indian beads and I realized I had forgotten my goal. I was too busy looking for beads, too consumed with finding the next one.

It's easy to be so intent on searching for blessings and accomplishments that we miss God in the process. Even though I had Indian beads to add to my collection, I felt disappointment for having missed out on more of what Weko Beach had to offer.

The biblical account of Mary and Martha is about misdirected focus. Mary chose to sit and hear Jesus, while Martha focused on the busy tasks at hand. She lost focus of what was really important. Time with Jesus is needed more than anything else.

Water is more important than Indian beads.

"But few things are needed—or indeed only one." – Luke 10:42

Put Your Feet Down

It made me laugh as I watched her first time with sand. As she was lowered down to stand in the sand, she held her feet up. She didn't want to touch it. It was something new, something she had never experienced before.

We get used to life and the things we are familiar with. Change isn't always easy, especially when it involves something we never experienced before. We refuse to put our feet into it. We become afraid of the unknown. It's human nature.

God knows every unfamiliar and new situation you run into. He wants you to trust Him. It's in those times He opens a door of opportunity to trust. He holds you as you set your feet down into each new situation. Just trust Him.

Put your feet down and start walking. God's got you covered.

"When I am afraid, I put my trust in You."
– Psalm 56:3

Beach Life

Some people swim in the lake. Some walk along the shore. Some lay on the beach catching the rays. Still some sit on the sand under umbrellas while others sit on benches farther away. But stop and think about it ... they are all there because of the water.

Our lives are all different. They are as different as the people along the beach. Not one is the same, but we are all where we are because of God.

Have you ever looked at your life and wished things were different? I have and I can bet most people have. You would rather be swimming than sitting on a beach. You are where you are because of God. He knew exactly where you would be today and what your life would be like. He is the potter shaping your life. You don't have to worry about it. Clay doesn't worry about the shape it takes; it just lets the potter do his thing.

Enjoy your beach life. It's exactly as it should be.

"Like clay in the hand of the potter, so are you in My hand." – Jeremiah 18:6

Not Interested

I looked at the stones. They were not appealing to me, and I was not interested. I couldn't care less. Maybe that was the lesson for the day.

None of us can be talented at everything. We become talented at what interests us. Our talents are driven by our interests. If we aren't interested, we don't take the time or make the effort. We keep on walking. It's like walking past the stones we aren't interested in and that's ok.

God made you the way you are. The abilities or talents you don't pick up along the way may become weaknesses at times, but that's all part of the plan. You need weaknesses. They turn you to God. When you don't have much to work with you rely on Him more. His Word becomes living truth. When I am weak, then I am strong.

Take an interest in uninteresting stones. They may become weaknesses causing you to delight in God.

"I delight in weaknesses. For when I am weak, then I am strong." – 2 Corinthians 12:10

Turn the Radio Up

I was a teenager who loved to spend my summer days on Weko Beach. Friends, a beach blanket, suntan oil, snacks, and a radio—I had it made. I'd turn on my favorite station and listen to the latest songs. The more I liked it, the louder it got.

Things change when we get older. We don't always express as loudly, or even at all, those things we like. Even when we feel something is important, we may not speak up. It's like turning down the volume on a radio at the beach so no one knows what we like or what we believe in.

I am no longer a teenager blaring today's latest hits. I've grown. I'm into contemporary Christian music now. I play with the idea of spending a day at the beach again— friends, a beach blanket, suntan oil, snacks, and ... music ... LOUD MUSIC ... music I am not ashamed of!

Turn the radio up. It may be your ministry!

"For I am not ashamed of the gospel, because it is the power of God that brings salvation to everyone who believes." – Romans 1:16

Top of the World

I stood there at the top of the boardwalk and looked out. It was exhilarating. I felt as if I were at the top of the world.

We find ourselves feeling much the same way when we reach our goals ... like we finally made it. We look out over all we have accomplished and see our success. It's tempting to take all the credit and to pat ourselves on the back for what we have accomplished. We may think we can handle anything and lose sight of Who really deserves the credit for our accomplishments.

You may be tempted at the height of success to take all the credit or to believe in yourself but remember Jesus when He was at the highest point of the temple. It was then that He was tempted by the devil yet He hung onto and used the Word of God to overcome the temptations at the top.

Beware of temptations at the top of the boardwalk. Stay in God's Word.

"Then the devil took Him to the holy city and had Him stand on the highest point of the temple."
– Matthew 4:5

Put Your Heart in It

I look forward to the beach. I look forward to walking along the shores of Lake Michigan each week. I enjoy it. I am where I want to be, doing what I want to do, and my heart is in it.

There are things in all of our lives that we have to do. Some things we do even though we don't want to while others we do because we want to.

God wants you. He doesn't want you to go through the motions without a heart for Him. The Bible talks of a day when you will worship Him in spirit. Your worship will be driven by a worshipping heart and not by rules or etiquette. That's like taking a walk on the beach because you want to, not because you have to. Your heart is into it. Your heart is near God.

Put your heart into it and find God along your walk.

"These people honor Me with their lips, but their hearts are far from Me." – Matthew 15:8

Walk On

It was a welcomed sight. The sun came out from behind the clouds. Although the summer was gone, the sunshine warmed me and encouraged me on.

Life's problems have a way of eating away at us and wearing us down. We can't see our way through to the other side of whatever we face and our hope disappears. It's like taking a walk on the beach and only seeing the clouds.

Are you facing days of uncertainty? Are your problems bigger than you? Are you losing hope? I've been there. I reached the point when nothing I could do would fix things. But in the midst of my most difficult struggles, God restored my hope. I don't know how He did it, but He lifted me up. Despair left and hope returned. My circumstances hadn't changed. I found His Word true: "plans to give you hope." He can and will do the same for you.

Walk on a cloudy day until the sun comes out again.

"For I know the plans I have for you, declares the Lord … plans to give you hope."
– Jeremiah 29:11

Stirred Up

The rough waves stirred up the sand along the water's edge. Sand could be seen mingled with Lake Michigan as if going through a blender.

Haven't we all asked "why" at some point? Why did this have to happen? Why has our peaceful life been disrupted like the sand stirred by the waves along the beach?

Just as Lake Michigan stirs up the sand, God may stir up your quiet, peaceful existence. If you read in Deuteronomy 32 about the eagle stirring up her nest, you can see the eagle does more than just that. She flutters over her young ones in the nest and bears them up on her wings.

God does the same thing. He may allow your life to be stirred up, but there is a purpose to it—a purpose you may not understand. He flutters over you and cares for you. He doesn't leave you alone but leads you through those stirred-up times.

Trust God in the mix of life.

"Like an eagle that stirs up its nest … the Lord alone led him." – Deuteronomy 32:11-12

Abundance of Beads

I saw it and kept walking. Yeah, it was an Indian bead and it would go with all the other beads in my collection, but I kept walking. When I first started collecting them, I would have picked it up. There was no way I would have left it there because I had so few. Why did I leave it? I have a lot now. It wasn't that I didn't appreciate the Indian bead, but I knew there were more where that came from.

We go through life worrying about bills or having food on the table. Why? We don't know where the money to pay for the bills will come from or how to take care of our families.

Jesus came to give life and not just life but an abundant life. That means you not only have what you need, you have an abundance of it. Those times when it is unclear how your needs will be met may very well be times when God is teaching you to trust in Him. When I walked past the Indian bead and left it, it was an act of trust, knowing there will be more in my future. Can you trust Jesus? He has an abundance of what you need.

"I have come that they may have life and have it to the full." - John 10:10

Sentimental Walks

I walked past the mom and her teenage son, remembering those days when my son and I walked along Weko Beach. I thought to myself, "In a few years, she will be thinking back on her walk with her son like I am now." I fought off the oncoming sentiments of yesterday's walks and continued along.

Time goes on. We can't stop it and for those of us who are sentimental, it can be a hard pill to swallow. Letting go of precious moments from the past and moving forward doesn't come easy for everyone.

Moving on doesn't mean you don't treasure those moments shared with someone else. It doesn't make them any less valuable. But by following Paul's advice and pressing on, you have the opportunity to make new memories. It's a way of letting go so that God remains first in your life.

Continue walking along the Water in spite of the sentiments.

"But one thing I do: Forgetting what is behind and straining towards what is ahead."
– Philippians 3:13

Cartwheels in the Sand

I watched the young girl as she playfully did cartwheels in the sand. It all seemed so carefree—so happy. She didn't seem to have a care in the world and, as young kids do, she soaked in the moment and enjoyed her time on the beach.

Although life is not always easy, we always have a choice as to how we are going to respond. Will we go through life sulking and not enjoying it because of unfair and harsh experiences? Or will we choose to soak up and enjoy the good experiences we run across during our lifetime?

A merry heart is good medicine. It does you good to let go of the unfair and hurtful experiences you have had and choose to simply enjoy the good ones. It is healing, rejuvenating your spirit. It is basking in the moments and enjoying what God has done. It is appreciating even the littlest of good you find here right now and flipping out over it.

Do a cartwheel in the sand. It will do you good.

"A cheerful heart is good medicine."
– Proverb 17:22

Do You Really Want It?

When I come across someone collecting stones along the beach, I figure they must really want it. If they didn't, they wouldn't take the time and energy to pick it up. They walk past the stones they don't want and pick up the ones they do.

We pass by our "stones" too. We let opportunities go to learn certain skills. We don't practice. We use our time on other things. If something is not important to us, we don't take the time for it. If something is important, we take the time to learn and practice it. Like stones picked up, we take the time and energy to practice what is important to us.

Where does God stand in your abilities? Are you using them for His purposes? Do you really want to? If you do, practice makes perfect. Take the time and energy to grow and develop your abilities to praise and worship Him with what you can do. Pick up the stones that pull you closer to God. It's worth it.

"Be diligent in these matters; give yourself wholly to them, so that everyone may see your progress." – 1 Timothy 4:15

Enjoying Your Weaknesses

When I was young, there were two things I would change about Weko Beach—the concrete filtration structure and the Cook Plant. Over the years, the filtration structure with its painted mural has become, in my mind, a "trademark" of Weko Beach. It sets the beach apart from others. The Cook Plant … well … I'm still working on that one. I still see it as a weakness, something I would change.

We see things in our lives we want to change. The change would bring beauty and strength. It would eliminate our weaknesses. But we aren't always able to change things. We learn to live with our weaknesses.

Behind every weakness lies power. While the Cook Plant is a weakness in my eyes, it has the ability to generate great power. God is the power behind your weaknesses. Your weakness gives Him the opportunity to show His power.

Enjoying your weakness is enjoying God's power.

"For Christ's sake, I delight in weaknesses. For when I am weak, then I am strong."
– 2 Corinthians 12:10

Life without a Leash

I probably walked past the sign a million times. It was posted along the dog paths leading to the beach. All dogs are required to remain on a 6' or less leash, but there always seems to be some dogs without one.

Rules, rules, and more rules. We get them everywhere we go. Traffic rules, family rules, "no shirt, no shoes, no service" rules, and ... worst of all ... IRS rules and regulations!

Rules don't always matter to people following after God and living life His way. Why? Most rules are in place to stop people from doing wrong things. When you follow God, you love the things He loves, and one of those things is righteousness—trying to do what's right. It's an inward mechanism Christians develop. You do things right not because it's a rule but simply because it is the right thing to do. It's what you want to do. It's like a dog off his leash. The leash doesn't matter because he already knows what to do.

Strive for life without a leash.

"Create in me a pure heart, O God, and renew a steadfast spirit within me." – Psalm 51:10

Distant Roar

I listened as I stood on the boardwalk. I could still hear the distant roar of the waves hitting the shores of Weko Beach down below. The sound was clear even here at the top.

We probably have all felt on our own and alone at times—separated from God. Our calling should never take us away from Him. No matter where we are, no matter what we do, we should always be able to hear Him.

When you can't hear God, what do you do? What can you do? If I can't hear the waves from the top of the boardwalk, I go back down to the water. I get nearer. Go back to God when you can't hear Him. Get back into the Word.

Wherever you are, listen. God is talking.

"For the Lord your God will be with you wherever you go." – Joshua 1:9

Past the Clouds

I sat up and looked to the sky. Even half asleep, tanning on the beach, I noticed the clouds blocking the sun. Thinking it would pass, I laid back down and waited for the sun to reappear.

Life can be going along just fine. Everything falls into place and goes our way ... until problems come like a cloud blocking the sun's rays.

When I looked up that day on the beach, I saw the clouds but I also saw the sun. Problems come. Don't deny the reality of them but see the hope too. God is there. Remember how He helped you in the past. If that isn't enough, remember how He helped others. Read how He helped the Israelites or how He helped people of the New Testament. You may have problems, but you also have hope.

Look past the clouds and see Hope.

"Come and see what God has done, His awesome deeds for mankind!" – Psalm 66:5

Toes

The footprint I was following was different. I studied it wondering if I was seeing right. One, two, three, four, five, six. This person had six toes.

We don't like being different. Usually we try to hide our differences for fear of being made fun of or of not being accepted. I think about the beachgoer with six toes. Most of us probably wouldn't take our shoes off even for a stroll on the beach.

How are you different from others? What differences do you hide? God created and gave life. He didn't mess up. The six-toed beachgoer got it right. He or she was comfortable enough to go barefoot on a public beach. Whatever differences you have, whether it's six toes or something else, God designed you that way. You are perfect.

Get comfortable. Take your shoes off and show your toes.

"The Spirit of God has made me; the breath of the Almighty gives me life." – Job 33:4

No Suit, No Problem

We went to the beach not expecting to swim. It was too early in the season, so we didn't wear our bathing suits. The water was still cold, but for us kids it didn't matter. After sticking our feet in and seeing others swimming, we wanted to go in too. My mom eventually suggested swimming with our t-shirts and shorts.

We work so hard at trying to get things just right but time and time again something messes it up. We see our imperfections. We don't measure up to those around us. In our minds, we are not ready. We have not earned the right. Maybe another day.

When life isn't perfect, when you've messed up for the umpteenth time, when you feel beneath those around you, you are ready. God accepts you right now just as you are. Life doesn't have to be perfect. You don't have to get things right. Come as you are.

The Water accepts all. No bathing suit, no problem.

"All those the Father gives Me will come to Me, and whoever comes to Me I will never drive away." – John 6:37

Necklaces

Sometime in July or early August, I would dump my jar of Indian beads onto the table. The kids and I would sort through them looking for ones that would make good necklaces. We looked for ones about the same size and with holes in the middle so we wouldn't have to drill open the center.   When the necklaces were done, the kids entered them in the county fair.

We all have blessings in our lives. They may be different, but we all have them. One of the greatest blessings is God's Word. It guides and teaches us at every age. It changes our hearts and our minds for the better.

My Indian beads represent words and ideas God had given me over the course of my walks along the beach— words and ideas that still mean a lot to me. I shared my Indian beads with my kids on those days to create necklaces to show in the fair.

Why not share what you hold in your heart with others? Bind them around your neck keeping them in sight for all to see.

"Bind them always on your heart; fasten them around your neck." – Proverb 6:21

Get Back Up

The way home led us through downtown Bridgman on sidewalks along the storefronts. Small side roads connected the surrounding neighborhoods to the town. A car pulled out unexpectedly from a side road hitting my friend and knocking her bike down. Luckily, she was okay. Only a few scratches.

When we reach a place in our relationship with God where we should be—total faith and trust in Him—we think we shouldn't have to go through anymore hardships. Spending time with God doesn't exclude you from problems. It's like spending a day at the beach. There is still trouble ahead.

Your relationship with God is important. Living His way and spending time with Him doesn't take you out of life's problems, but it does help you through them. People who don't follow God rely on something else, but that something else may not hold them up when the next problem comes along. Spend time with God. He helps you get back up.

"For though the righteous fall seven times, they rise again, but the wicked stumble when calamity strikes." – Proverb 24:16

Up or Down

When I reached the top of Old Baldy, I accomplished what I had set out to do. I enjoyed the view for a little while before heading back down. Truth is, I never really wanted to go back down after the hard climb up, but my sisters and my brother raced to the bottom. It was easier running down than climbing up.

We are human with the human tendency to sin. It's that tendency to do wrong even when we want to do the right thing. It's a struggle that has gone on since the time of Adam and Eve.

It's easier to run down a dune than it is to climb up. It's easier to follow human nature running with the crowd than it is to take the higher road and stand your ground. It's a lot like not wanting to run down Old Baldy but doing it anyway.

Standing at the top of the dune is better than running down it.

"For what I want to do I do not do, but what I hate I do." – Romans 7:15

Skipping Conditions 1

Some days I can skip a stone along the water's surface. Today was not one of those days. I tried but the stone hit the water and it was over. Why? Waves. The water was too wavy. It would not allow me to skip the stone.

There are things we attempt to do. We may have all the talent in the world and yet we still fail. We try and try again but it makes no difference. It's like trying to skip a stone on a wavy Lake Michigan. It goes nowhere and it's not going to go anywhere because of the waves.

You may have your goals set, but it is God who works the outcome. Just as the water is a condition for a successful skip, God is the ingredient of success in your goals. He is the One who works all the varying factors out to succeed. Talent isn't enough.

Consider the Water before you skip your stone.

"In Him who works out everything in conformity with the purpose of His will..." – Ephesians 1:11

Skipping Conditions 2

I lost count. The flat stone bounced across Lake Michigan skipping so many times it was hard to count. I threw the next stone, but it only bounced a few times. It wasn't as flat as the first one, leaving me to think that was the reason for the few skips.

Ability is important when we attempt things. Many times, we get caught up with looking at the outcome that we miss the ability it takes to arrive at the outcome. That can be a source of frustration when we try to do something and it doesn't work. We need ability.

You can set your goals, but God still works out the outcome. He provides you the ability to accomplish your goal. Just as the flat stone skipped more than the stone not quite so flat, God provides your talent and determines how far that talent will go. Your God-given talents are an ingredient to your goals.

"In Him who works out everything in conformity with the purpose of His will..." – Ephesians 1:11

Skipping Conditions 3

I don't skip stones every time I walk along Weko Beach. In fact, most days I don't. I guess it's because I like to walk more. If I am interested in skipping a stone on my walk, I skip it.

Along with our ability, there has to be a desire. Without it, our abilities probably won't get used. It's like the days I don't feel like skipping stones. I know how to skip a stone but because I don't want to, I don't. On days I do feel like skipping stones, I do.

You have your goals. You have God. You have the ability. Now you need the desire. God orchestrates all of it—the circumstances, the abilities, and the desire. He gives you the desire for your goals. Do what you can and leave the outcome with Him.

Skip your stone and watch God pull it all together.

"In Him who works out everything in conformity with the purpose of His will..." – Ephesians 1:11

Up, Down

The boardwalk went up the dune and leveled out at the top before heading back down.

We reach the top and think we should be able to continue our climb up. We get disappointed and maybe even angry when we can go no farther. Everything seems like it is downhill from there. We all have those seasons. Maybe we get laid off. Maybe it was the end of a relationship. Maybe life just became stagnant. Whatever the situation, we feel like it was the beginning of the end.

You don't have to be discouraged in those times. God is in control even in the downhill times. The Bible clearly tells us that God is the One who lifts people up and brings them down. He knows what He is doing, and His plan is perfect.

Trust God. He decides when you walk up the boardwalk and when you walk down.

"It is God who judges: He brings one down, He exalts another." – Psalm 75:7

Sunscreen

We arrived for an afternoon of sun and fun. It wasn't even noon yet and it was already hot. The sun was in full power. Not wanting any regrets, I immediately got out the sunscreen.

We want to enjoy life. We want to be out in the sun, enjoying the fun. But too much sun and fun without any sunscreen brings regrets later on.

Keeping a healthy, well-balanced perspective on the fun of life can avoid regrets down the road. But how do you do that? You put Son-screen on. When you follow God, there is protection from getting burned. The deceptive fun of life threatening to burn you up is still there, but with God you are able to walk through without being set on fire. His way blocks out the heat and future regrets.

No regrets when you put on Son-screen.

"When you walk through the fire, you will not be burned; the flames will not set you ablaze."
— Isaiah 43:2

Join the Class

It was another Wednesday morning on Weko Beach as I finished my walk on the north end. I could hear the sounds of music and the class instructor's voice as I passed the Beach Town Grill. The exercise class was in full swing. Maybe I should join?

There are many of us—me included—who think we can keep on track with God. We try to go it alone much like exercising on our own.

Others serve a purpose in your relationship with God. Every one of us faces struggles at times. I normally try to handle my problems on my own, but there came a time when the situations I faced were too big for me. I needed others.

God places people in your life to help you, to lean on in troubled times, to provide clear advice in confusing times, and simply to steer you away from mistakes. Your Christians friends are there to help you live out—exercise—your faith. Join the class. Exercise faith. Grow.

"As iron sharpens iron, so one person sharpens another." – Proverb 27:17

A High-Tide Day

The tides of Lake Michigan can have a big effect on where I walk along the beach. My search for Indian beads is dependent on the tide too. High-tide days are not good for collecting Indian beads. But when the tide is low, the water can leave pebbles and Indian beads on the sand in my path.

We can't always see God at work. We find ourselves in the middle of something and wonder where God is and why in the world we are here right in the middle of it all. It's like going to Weko Beach on a high tide day—we can't see the Indian beads.

God has His way. You are right where you should be right when you should be there. He lets you see what you need to see when you need to see it. Trust Him.

God works His perfect way on high-tide days too.

"Trust in the Lord with all your heart and lean not on your own understanding; in all your ways submit to Him, and He will make your paths straight." – Proverbs 3:5-6

July

"Build your castle with God's blueprint."

Get Your Head Wet

The beach was a new experience for my daughter, and I was eager for her to enjoy it to the fullest. I encouraged her to get into the water. "Get your head wet." Of course, I meant for her to go under, but kids do the sweetest yet unexpected things sometimes. She did get her head wet but not the way I was thinking. She bent over and stuck her head in the shallow water.

Don't we do the same thing with God? We think it's enough to have the head knowledge without experiencing anymore. It feels safe. We don't know what God will bring into our lives or what He will ask of us. We think the more we know about Him the more we have a relationship with Him.

You can know a lot about a person and still not have a personal relationship with them. All the knowledge in the world about God won't bring the "personal" in unless you let Him have His place in your thoughts and actions. That's experiencing Him beyond head knowledge.

"Here I am! I stand at the door and knock. If anyone hears My voice and opens the door, I will come in" — Revelations 3:20

Longer Walks

If you have ever been to Weko Beach, most people stay near the Beach Town Grill and the parking lot. They spread out as far as the stream that empties out into Lake Michigan, but usually not much farther. Since I was coming up empty-handed, I decided to walk south of the stream. If there are other beachgoers collecting Indian beads like me, maybe they didn't venture that far. It paid off. I found a few Indian beads.

Just like the beachgoers at Weko Beach, most of us want to take the easy shorter routes through life. We want to stay where it's not so hard to turn back and where the conveniences of life are. But it's in going the distance and taking the walks less travelled we find our blessings. When taking the longer narrow walk God leads us on, we find our greatest blessing—a relationship with Him.

How does a long walk on a less-travelled beach sound?

"But small is the gate and narrow the road that leads to life, and only a few find it."
— Matthew 7:14

Building a Castle

Ever since I was young I wanted to build a picture-perfect castle. No matter how hard I tried, it never came close to the picture in my head. Walls would collapse. Water would wash part of it away. And the design ... well ... it looked more like what it was—an upside-down bucket of sand, not a castle.

Most of us want a good, "picture-perfect" life. Try as we might, it never works out that way. Things happen causing it to collapse or wash away. Even if that doesn't happen, our lives still seem upside down like a bucket of sand.

Jesus tells us how to build our lives up by hearing and living His way. It doesn't mean the water won't come or things won't collapse. What He does tell us is the structure will be better—more sound. The foundation will be solid. You will be able to take the onslaught of collapsing walls and rushing water. Be wise. Build your castle with His blueprint.

"Everyone who hears these words of Mine and puts them into practice is like a wise man who built his house upon the rock."
– Matthew 7:24

No Matter the Generation

You couldn't help but notice them. They strolled contently along Weko Beach hand-in-hand as if they were teenagers. In reality, they could have been the oldest couple there. I watched as they walked, and I wondered, *"Did they start walking the beach a long time ago?"* They must have found some benefit all those years ago to still be walking today.

Every once in awhile, I run across this idea that God and the Bible are no longer relevant. What was good for yesterday isn't good for today.

Truth is, the benefits you get from following God and His Word are the same today as they were back when that old couple started walking Weko Beach. Society changes, but God does not. His Word is truth and truth doesn't change regardless of the generation you live in.

God is relevant no matter the generation.

"Jesus Christ is the same yesterday and today and forever." – Hebrews 13:8

Why Stones?

My feet weren't too happy as I walked on the stones along the beach. I thought to myself, "Why did God make stones on the beach? Why couldn't there just be sand and water?" Forget the stones—we don't need them.

Sometimes we wonder about things like that. Why doesn't God just work life out for us? There would be no need for abilities because God would take care of everything.

The Bible tells of a time Jesus healed a blind man. He told the man to go to the pool of Siloam and wash. Jesus could have healed him right then and there, but He had the blind man go to the pool for healing. Why? Maybe it was an opportunity to show faith. By using his ability to walk, he had the opportunity to show his faith in Jesus by doing what he could do. Jesus had the blind man walk—probably over stones—to do his part as a show of faith.

Take a walk of faith over your stones.

"Go...wash in the pool of Siloam. So the man went and washed, and came home seeing."
— John 9:7

The Broken Shovel

After emptying our toy bag, we discovered the shovel was broken. We had to come up with an alternative way to scoop up the sand for the castle we were about to build. For a while we dug with our hands. It worked a little bit, but a shovel would have worked so much better.

Some situations look impossible to us. We go over it again and again in our minds trying to come up with a way to solve it. Nothing makes any sense and yet we aren't ready to walk away in defeat. We don't have the answers or the tools we need.

When you have tough circumstances with no solution in sight, it's ok. God has the answer and tools. He knows when and how to handle your situation. Our problem was solved that day when we found a shovel left behind by an earlier beachgoer.

Sometimes you just have to let things be until God hands you a shovel.

"With God all things are possible."
— Matthew 19:26

Save the Dunes

There is a sign along the boardwalk at Weko Beach. It says something about saving the dunes by walking on the boardwalk. The sign clearly is there to take care of the dunes.

Decisions. Decisions. Decisions. Life is made up of decisions. Those decisions can have a positive impact or they can have a negative impact. It's up to us. What we decide can start something on the right path or send it on a downward spiral. We can choose to save the dune or wear it down by walking on it.

Your decisions are important but, when it comes to this world, Jesus already did the saving. Your decisions are not going to undo what He has already done. When you follow your calling, it should have a positive effect on others … like saving the dune by staying on the boardwalk. Who knows the impact of what you do and whether it will inspire others towards Christ.

Follow the boardwalk for the good of others.

"Not looking to your own interests but each of you to the interests of others." – Philippians 2:4

City Workers

It was mid-October as I walked along the boardwalk. I changed course to avoid getting in the way of the city workers. They were there fixing the displaced boards.

We don't always know what goes on behind the scenes. That thought occurred to me as I considered the city workers fixing the boardwalk. Most of the summer beachgoers probably don't even give a second thought about the beach's upkeep.

At twelve years old, Jesus met with a group of teachers studying the Word. They didn't receive any recognition in the Bible and yet they were used by God to impart knowledge and help Jesus grow in His relationship with Him. Just like the city workers' contributions, the teachers got overlooked but their contributions to Jesus' upbringing was not any less valuable.

Your goals and successes aren't measured by how much recognition you receive, but by doing what God has put you here to do.

"After three days they found Him in the temple courts, sitting among the teachers, listening to them and asking them questions." – Luke 2:46

Where are the Clouds?

I started packing up. The clouds gathered and the clear skies disappeared. It was time to head home. The sun was not coming back out.

Sometimes we lose our way when we face hard situations. We can't see through the problems, and the ending is nowhere in sight. It's like endless clouds blocking our sun on a summer day. There seems to be no point in staying. They aren't going away.

Are you under clouds feeling like they are there to stay? There is hope. Clouds blow away with the wind and the sun comes out again. Fix your eyes on God. You can't see Him, but He is there and it's the unseen that lasts, not the seen.

Soon you will be asking, "Where are the clouds?"

"We fix our eyes not on what is seen, but on what is unseen, since what is seen is temporary, but what is unseen is eternal."
– 2 Corinthians 4:18

A One-Eighty

I don't know much about the waters of Lake Michigan. For example, why do waves flow one way one day and the next day, it's the opposite?

Situations don't always make sense to us. We look at things and think we have it all figured out until something unexpected happens. It's like walking on Weko Beach expecting the waves to flow the same way but finding them doing a one-eighty.

I never took the time to figure out why waves flow one way and the next day they flow another. The reasons don't matter to me. I trust God. When you find yourself in situations that don't make sense … when God seems to be doing a one-eighty or He seems to be doing things wrong … maybe understanding His reasons doesn't matter as much as trusting in Him does. He is God. He has the power, the wisdom, and the love to do what He wants for your good.

In one-eighty situations, trust is more valuable than understanding.

"See, I am doing a new thing! Now it springs up; do you not perceive it?"—Isaiah 43:19

Small and Broken

Really? The Indian beads I came across fell short of what I was looking for. First, there was the small one I found. I was looking for that mother of all beads. Then this … a damaged broken one. It reminded me of much of my life at the moment.

We have seasons in our lives when things don't measure up to our expectations. Others are getting the big elusive blessings, while still others are getting the perfect marriage, perfect family, perfect job, perfect life … and we see ourselves with a small or broken life. It hurts.

I went home with my small and broken beads after asking God why. I had to learn to be thankful for whatever blessings God gave me whether it was a small, broken life or a big, perfect life. I learned from the brokenness and the smallness I was going through.

You can be thankful in the small, broken seasons of your life because God is teaching you valuable lessons.

"Give thanks in all circumstances; for this is God's will for you in Christ Jesus"
—1 Thessalonians 5:18

The Unknowing Pilot

I was questioning my decision. I had been going through a very difficult time and found myself at the beach trying to sort things through. "God, if this is what I should do, can You let me know? I need some affirmation … something unusual. I don't know what—maybe a plane flying low along the shoreline or something?"

Sometimes we don't know what to do. We struggle trying to come up with the answers and then, when we do have them, we still question it.

God can use others to affirm the decisions you make and they may not even know it. When Abraham's servant went to find Isaac's wife, he asked God for affirmation. The girl who offered to water his camels would be the one. Rebekah offered to water the camels not knowing she was giving the servant God's affirmation.

A small plane flew above me and continued its course along the shoreline. Decision made.

"Drink, and I'll water your camels too."
— Genesis 24:14

Trickle of Sand

The sand started to dry out on what I called my sand castle. Some of it started to give way and fall. I headed to the water with my bucket, hoping I could stop the trickling of sand that threatened to break down my castle. By the time I got back, a big section of my castle was down.

It's a common mistake we make, thinking a little bit of this or a little bit of that won't really matter. After all it's such a small amount. What harm could it do? But as the tiny trickle of sand led to bigger damage in my castle, so the tiny amount of wrong in our lives can lead to bigger problems. God warns us about that.

You can avoid this mistake by staying in tune with Jesus. It's like keeping a sand castle wet so it doesn't have a chance to dry out and cause more damage.

Stop the trickle effect. Stay in the Word.

"Don't you know that a little yeast leavens the whole batch of dough?"
- 1 Corinthians 5:6

Singing Stones

I couldn't get the song out of my head. It was there all day and as I walked along the beach, it still played in my head. I wanted to sing it out loud but walking along a public beach with a lot of people around and a voice not quite in tune made me think twice. I let the song play inside my head and that's where it stayed.

We all get a song stuck in our head. It rewinds and rewinds singing out its tune all the while. Jesus's disciples had a day where they sang praises to Him so much that the Pharisees complained. Jesus replied, "If the disciples didn't sing out, the stones would."

You may be like me and not have an awesome singing voice, but you do have talent. Our talents should sing out to and about Jesus. Even if you don't have a perfect voice, you do have something you can do that will sing out your praises to Him.

Let your stones sing out!

"If they keep quiet, the stones will cry out."
— Luke 19:40

The Ugly Piping

It was ugly and stuck out like a sore thumb. Piping used for gutters around a house. I don't know how it got there, but a portion of it was buried deep enough it couldn't be moved.

It's not unusual for us to bury our faults and our scars. We try to hide them from each other to make us seem whole and well again. It never works though. They run so deep nothing in life can really bury them for good. It's like the ugly gutter piping I found on Weko Beach, partially buried but not totally hidden.

God heals your scars and loves you inspite of your faults. You don't have to hide them from Him. He accepts you as you are. Admitting them is the first step towards healing. It is a step of growth in your relationship with Him. It's refreshing when what you have been hiding so long is now out there in the open with God and you discover that ...

He loves you anyway.

"Repent, then, and turn to God, so that your sins may be wiped out, that times of refreshing may come from the Lord." – Acts 3:19

Why Am I Here?

I looked at the people around me wondering why they were here. I knew why I was here. No doubt they were here for different reasons.

We follow God and seek Him out for different reasons. It could be for comfort, for protection, for guidance. It could be to praise and thank Him for what He has done. It's like the scene at Weko Beach. We all come for different reasons.

When I consider all that is going on in my life and how much help I need from God and then add everyone else's needs, I can't understand how God can handle it all. You and I can be assured that God can handle everything. He doesn't get worn out from it, and it's not too much for Him to handle. He gave His Word. One of the purposes of the Bible is to help.

God has a Word for why you are here. Dig in.

"All Scripture is God-breathed and is useful for teaching, rebuking, correcting and training in righteousness." – 2 Timothy 3:16

Broken Boardwalk

The boardwalk stopped in the middle of its path but continued about twenty feet later. There was a yellow ribbon connecting the two ends of the boardwalk. It had broken down.

We are called to certain purposes in each of our lives. The beginning is exciting and nothing can keep us from it. It's interesting the boardwalk had broken high up on the dune. We can be at the top of our game right where we are called to be and break down. Mistakes, poor judgement, broken boardwalks happen even at the height of our calling. But God offers us a fix.

When you get off track and your boardwalk is broken, there is hope. Jesus tells you to repent and turn back to Him. Say you are sorry, decide to turn from whatever made you mess up, and go back to God. That's called repentance. Just as I saw the other end of the boardwalk …

God can get you past the broken boardwalk when you repent.

"Repent, then, and turn to God."
— Acts 3:19

Fallen Leaves

Fall had arrived at Weko Beach. The leaves changed their color and began to fall one by one. A few fallen leaves landed in the gentle waves rolling back and forth.

Change comes. It's inevitable like the leaves changing each fall in Michigan. It disrupts our lives forcing us to change along with it.

With every change comes opportunity for growth. Each change may force changes in different areas of your life, but each one should move you toward a greater trust in God. The Bible talks of one delighting and meditating in God. He will be like a tree where his leaf doesn't wither. It doesn't change color and fall to the ground.

Maybe God has allowed things to change in your life which forced you to trust in Him. It's like letting the fallen leaves float into the gentle hands of God as you trust Him.

Can you trust the Water with your fallen leaves?

"That person is like a tree … whose leaf does not wither." – Psalm 1:3

The Cover of the Book

I'm guilty of judging people at the beach by the books they read.

We all have been touched by the comments and opinions of people who don't think too much of God. For whatever reason, they have turned away.

"Don't judge a book by its cover." Think about it. Isn't that what happens when people pass judgement on Christians? Christians are the church—the cover of God. We mess up just like unbelievers and it's ugly. Unbelievers don't see the difference and they turn away, only seeing the hypocrisy. But what if judgement would pause and wait until it's past the cover and into the Book? They would find a beautiful God in all His perfection. No hypocrisy, no sin. They would find their judgement of sinful Christians was projected onto a perfect God.

The cover of a book doesn't always represent what's inside.

"Follow God's example, therefore, as dearly loved children." – Ephesians 5:1

Follow the Sound

I love the sound of waves. It's gentle. It's calming and comforting. It replaces the urgent demands of responsibilities. It's a sound I look forward to after a hectic day.

From urgent demands placed on us by our jobs to the necessary needs of our families, there never seems to be an opportune time to just sit back and listen to the gentle sound of the waves.

The world misleads you to think time spent listening instead of doing is not valuable. Our world is a world centered on accomplishments. Just as the sounds of the waves calmed my overworked and broken spirit, time spent listening to God—hearing His Voice—is healing. It becomes a voice we recognize and love, a voice we go to for help in the day-to-day demands and pressures of life.

Whether it's in the sound of the waves or something else, listen for God and follow the sound.

"And His sheep follow Him because they know His voice." – John 10:4

My Favorite Bead

After every walk, I pull my new Indian beads out of my pocket and look at them. I have a ritual of picking out my favorite one. What one is the largest? Is it perfectly round? How is the condition of it? Those are the things I look at—the size, shape, and condition—things I can see.

Aren't we glad God doesn't judge us that way? It doesn't matter to Him what our size or shape is. He doesn't care what condition we are in. Maybe that's because He knows what He can do with us regardless of those things. He sees our value and it's on the inside ... in our hearts.

It may be the Indian beads that were not my favorite came with a greater value—a lesson I needed to hear more than what a perfect Indian bead could teach.

Don't judge a bead by its appearance. Look at what it's taught you.

"People look at the outward appearance, but the Lord looks at the heart." – 1 Samuel 16:7

Quit Walking

I wasn't up for a walk on Weko Beach. I was lucky to even be here. I sat tired and broken.

When life hits us so hard, we struggle. We use all we have to come up with answers. We do what we can to soothe our pain, but it still hurts to the core. We are tired and broken.

You may be having days when life is hitting you hard. You feel tired and broken. You don't have it in you to continue walking. I understand. I reached that point myself. That is the time to stop walking and sit in the presence of God. That is the time to allow God to do what you cannot do and to trust in His plan for your life. His plans are good even if they are different from what you had in mind. Sometimes God just wants us to connect with Him and let Him take care of those things that are wearing you out and breaking you down.

When life hits hard, quit walking. Just sit on the beach.

"Be still and know that I am God."
— Psalm 46:10

Together

I walked along Weko Beach wondering about the direction of my life. Along the way I passed someone's rendition of a sandcastle. It was holding up pretty well given its condition and the environment it was in. I wish I could hold up like that.

The situations we find ourselves in can be a real struggle. It can be hard to deal with them and we may not have what it takes to hold up under them. We want to be like that sandcastle, to hold up under menacing winds that could blow us away, and to stand firm when passing beachgoers could walk all over us knocking us down. Circumstances leave us feeling threatened.

God keeps things together when you can't. He knows and has the abilities you don't have to hold your circumstances and you together.

Hang on to the One who holds it together.

"And in Him all things hold together."
– Colossians 1:17

Old Concrete

Along the beach are stones that look like old pieces of concrete. I notice them because over time Indian beads have gotten stuck in them. I want the Indian beads but because it is stuck to the concrete stone, I leave it. I don't see the value in it.

Haven't we had conversations with people we think don't know what they are talking about? As a teenager and a young woman, I had those same thoughts about older people. We look at them and they seem stuck in life. We draw the wrong conclusions thinking they don't know as much as we do, and that's why they are where they are.

The older generation is full of wisdom. Why? Because of length of days, they have lived life. They have lived and learned a lot of what the younger generations are just now going through. They have developed wisdom and an understanding that only comes by living life. It's like an old piece of concrete with an Indian bead stuck in it. Some blessings only come with time.

"Is not wisdom found among the aged? Does not long life bring understanding?" – Job 12:12

The Source

They were outnumbered by far. You could tell they hadn't expected the whole flock of sea gulls to gather near them as they threw the bread crumbs.

When we need something, where do we go? Who do we turn to? It's usually ourselves. We turn to what we know. We turn to what we have. We rely on ourselves—on what we can do. It's not a bad thing to do for yourself what you can do, but why is it that God almost always seems to be the last place we turn to when dealing with anything?

The flock of sea gulls knew who was throwing out the bread crumbs. They instinctively went to the source. Out of all the people on the beach that day, they knew which hand the bread crumbs came from.

Remember all the blessings you have. Remember all the difficult times you have overcome. Remember all the love and all the hope. Remember the Source.

"You open Your hand and satisfy the desires of every living thing." – Psalm 145:16

The Highest SPF

My kids complained when I picked out a high SPF lotion at the store before going to the beach, but I'm not alone. Families come to the beach and one of the first things they do is put on protection.

Life has a way of making it seem like anything and everything could happen. It becomes an impossible balancing act to protect yourself and your family from everything that could go wrong. The protection we do put into place may not protect from whatever happens next.

There is no better protection in life for you or your family than God. He has all you need to protect from every unforeseen problem. He is capable in all life's problems. There is no limit to what He can do. Handling your problems without Him is like using a low SPF lotion. It may be ok one day, but on a high UIV day it can't do the job.

Use the Highest SPF for all your sun-burning days.

"The Lord will keep you from all harm—He will watch over your life." – Psalm 121:7

Hanging On

I'm thankful for railings, especially the higher I get. I hung on to them as I climbed the boardwalk. It steadied me both physically and emotionally. Railings are a good thing.

As we go along in life, how do we go? How do we handle things in good times and in bad times? How do we handle the uphill climb? Do we hang onto the railings along the way or do we go it alone without anything to steady us?

I'm so thankful for God's Word. It is the railing in my life that steadies me when I face a tall dune. It has the promises I hang onto when I am unsure of myself and I can't see how to work things out. It is what I hang on to when something is too much for me—bigger than I am.

God has your back. He offers His Word to you to steady you, both physically and emotionally. It's what you hang onto when there is nothing left to hang on to.

Hold on to the railing. It's a good thing.

"But test them all; hold onto what is good."
– 1 Thessalonians 5:21

A Morning Walk

I listened to the soft, gentle roll of the waves and felt the warm sun on my back. I don't often walk on the beach this early in the day, but today I took in the new morning on Lake Michigan.

We don't always receive change well. It may be because something good is changing and we want to hang on to it. It may be that the change is bringing something bad. It may scare us because of the uncertainty. It's in those times we need hope.

You are not alone. The Bible tells of God's unending love and His faithfulness towards you. It shows in new ways every day. It shows itself in a morning walk on a Michigan beach whispering soft, gentle encouragement and shining hope along your path. You have hope because God is in charge, because He is by your side, and simply because He is who He is.

Renew your hope in Him. Go for a morning walk.

"Because of the Lord's great love, we are not consumed, for His compassions never fail. They are new every morning; great is Your faithfulness."—Lamentations 3:22-24

Sandbar Limits

One of the boundaries my mom set for us kids when swimming in Lake Michigan was the sandbar. You could see it from the edge of the water. It seemed far away. To get to it, we had to swim through deep water that was not over our heads.

When you can't see beyond your circumstances, God does. When you don't understand, God does. You may be limited in your understanding. You may be limited in what you see.

But God is a great God. His understanding goes deeper than the sandbars or even the waters to get to the sandbar. What comfort and reassurance knowing that God has understanding way beyond your limits. My mom set limits based on what we could handle, but be thankful ...

God's limits go past the sandbar.

"Great is our Lord and mighty in power; His understanding has no limit."—Psalm 147:5

Catch the Wind

I watched as my kids ran up and down the beach with a kite barely hanging in the air. They were trying so hard to get it to catch the wind and fly.

Hopes and dreams. We all have them. When we are young, we dare to run with them, to see them catch the wind and fly.

God gives you the desires of your heart. When I look at this, I'm thinking this could be interpreted two different ways. First, God gave you the desire—the will, the want. Second, God fulfills your desire. There is never a good reason to give up on your hopes and dreams when you have God. He created you and your desires. They are from Him. Everything is His. He has the resources to fulfill those desires. Giving up, then, is actually giving up on God. He can and will do what you desire. Write "it" down. Keep "it" in focus. And run with "it". That's all He requires.

Run until the Wind catches "it."

"May He give you the desire of your heart and make all your plans succeed." – Psalm 20:4

Counting My Beads

Another part of my ritual after every walk is to pull my new Indian beads out of my pocket and count them. I count them all whether they are my favorites or not. Big or small, perfect or imperfect—they are counted. Then as I place them in my jar, I see and I am reminded of my beads from the past.

Counting our blessings has a way of reminding us of the past and what God has taught us and pulled us through. It re-enforces our faith in His love and His desire to help us. We remember how we faced impossible odds and, looking back, we are amazed at how those impossibilities worked out. We know it was not us who pulled it off but God.

Counting your blessings is a faith-building exercise encouraging you on with more confidence in a loving and caring God who is willing to help with life's impossibilities.

Take time to count your Indian beads.

"Do you still not understand ... remember the five loaves for the five thousand, and how many basketfuls you gathered?"
— Matthew 16:9

August

"We all need a Lifeguard."

Drifting Away

I listened as the mom swung her arms and yelled at her kids to come back to the water in front of her. The waves carried my siblings and I farther down the beach and my mom would do the same thing. I did the same with my kids too. I wanted them to stay in front of me where I could see them and they were close.

Life is like that. Our kids grow up and go their own way. We want to keep them close and we may not be happy about them going off in their own direction. It's like they have drifted away.

God has a plan for everyone, including your kids, and it may not be what you had in mind. He knows better than you. The way I see it, if they are in God's plan, be happy about it. That's better than being in your plan and out of His any day.

Sometimes the drifting is part of God's plan.

"For I know the plans I have for you … to prosper you and not to harm you, plans to give you hope and a future." – Jeremiah 29:11

Throw It Back

It looked like an Indian bead. It was round and had what seemed to be the center of a bead. I bent down and picked it up only to find it wasn't. It was a small, round pebble with dirt in the middle. I threw it into the water.

Isn't life like that? At first glance, something seems good. We see certain attributes leading us to believe in its goodness. Maybe it's well-rounded or well-centered. Only when we get farther into it do we see it for what it really is.

The Bible tells you to beware of false prophets who mislead you by disguising themselves. You can be misled by many things that seem like blessings but are not. People, jobs, situations, products—you name it. What do you do when that happens?

If it's not a blessing, throw it back.

"Watch out for false prophets. They come to you in sheep's clothing, but inwardly they are ferocious wolves." – Matthew 7:15

Good for Soles

I have this funny notion that walking in the sand is good for the soles of my feet. Don't know where I picked up the idea. Probably from some commercial selling a product for foot care. The whole idea centers on the sand smoothing the roughness of my feet. Funny, but maybe there is some truth to it?

Life offers all of us some rough spots. We get down during those times and we don't want to walk through them. But everything happens for a reason. God allows the rough spots to refine and smooth away the dead, useless areas of our lives. He uses them to show us where hope comes from.

Just as I walk along Weko Beach in the hopes of getting good sole care, you can walk through the rough spots in your life knowing God is caring for your soul. Put your hope in Him!

Souls are conditioned by walking through the rough spots. That's where hope is renewed.

"Why, my soul, are you downcast? Why so disturbed within me? Put your hope in God."
— Psalm 42:11

Taken Back

The water was wavy. I was just about to pick up this stone when the waves came and took it away. I was right there. I had it in my hand. It was mine and yet the water took it back. I felt a little robbed.

Don't we have times when we feel robbed by God? He allows us to have something and then takes it back. As I grow older, I'm finding I can't do some of the things that I was able to do when I was young. It can be frustrating.

You may not understand why God gives you talents for a time and then takes them away. He knows what He is doing. Trusting God and putting Him first allows you to live life on different terms. It's an opportunity to refocus. You can bless God even when you have lost the ability to do what you could do before.

Bless the water when it takes your stone back.

"The Lord gave, and the Lord has taken away; may the name of the Lord be praised." – Job 1:21

Lifeguard on Duty

Sometimes I wonder if a lifeguard on Weko Beach would be a good idea. I picture a weathered lifeguard station occupied by a person steadily watching over the swimmers in the water.

Life can be hard. It can be intimidating. If you're like me, there are days when you need all the help you can get … someone who has your back … someone watching out for you like a lifeguard on the beach.

One of the promises in the Bible is that Jesus will never leave you. He is on duty watching out for you as you live life. It's His job. When people choose to live life without Jesus, they are choosing to go it alone without His help. Lifeguards specialize in saving people from drowning and pulling them back to safety. Jesus is the only One who knows the dangers of this life and the only One who can pull you back to safety.

Why not choose life with the Lifeguard on Duty?

"The Lord watches over you." – Psalm 121:5

Lifeguards & First Aid Kits

Where there is a lifeguard, there is also a first aid kit. Lifeguards keep them on hand. Should the need arise, they are prepared and know how to use it.

Life comes with its bumps and bruises. Some hurts go deep and require stitches. Still others go even deeper, requiring a stay at the hospital.

There is one recorded incident after another of Jesus healing someone. He is not physically here with you as He was back in biblical times, but you can still go to Him for healing. He has everything you need to heal even your deepest wounds. His Word acts as healing ointment for your soul. His Word rids you of infectious bad attitudes like Bactine preventing infections from an open sore. His Word covers you as a band-aid covers a wound until healing comes.

Jesus is the Lifeguard with a first aid kit—ready to use.

"Lord my God, I called to You for help, and You healed me." – Psalm 30:2

Lifeguards & Megaphones

As lifeguards watch over swimmers from their stations, they may see a potential problem and shout out warnings over their megaphones.

Good advice. Red flags. Warnings. Some choose to listen and pay attention to them. Others ignore them and find themselves in bad situations. It's like swimming in Lake Michigan and choosing to pay attention or to ignore the shout out from the lifeguard.

Jesus loves you. He puts people with good advice in your life. He gives you a conscience to know right from wrong. He guides you with the Bible. You have a Savior shouting out good advice, waving red flags, sending warnings. Some may think Jesus and the Bible are foolish, but you know better. Jesus's way of life and the Bible are instructions to guide us away from hurtful and dangerous situations.

Hear His Megaphone. What will you do?

"I will instruct you and teach you in the way you should go; I will counsel you with My loving eye on you." – Psalm 32:8

Lifeguards & Fitness

Lifeguards probably have to keep fit. At a moment's notice, they have to be able to run, swim, carry.

We don't know what's going to happen. So many times, we assume life will always be the way it is today even though we know that isn't how it works. We need to be ready just as a lifeguard is ready for anything at the beach.

I read something once during a tragedy I was going through that cemented in my mind the importance of being ready. We think we can turn to God during troubled times and turn our faith on when we need it. Faith isn't a button you can press on and off when needed. It's more like a muscle needing regular exercise. It needs a regular workout. So how do you do that? You turn to the Word every day ... whether you face problems or not. When the big problems come, turning to God and His Word has become a way of life.

Schedule a fitness plan today.

"Man shall not live on bread alone, but on every word that comes from the mouth of God."
— Matthew 4:4

Lifeguards & Swimming

Ever meet a lifeguard who doesn't know how to swim? I haven't. Swimming is part of the job description.

Following God is no different. We have to know His Word and how to put it into action like a lifeguard who knows how to swim and puts it into action when the time comes.

The Bible tells us God's Word is alive and active. It comes to life through the choices we make. It comes alive when we live it out. We can't live out the Word of God if we don't know what it involves. When we know His Word, it changes us. It makes us look at ourselves. The wrong is divided from the right. Following God means staying in the Word and using it when the occasion arises.

Learn to swim with His Word.

"For the word of God is alive and active. Sharper than any double-edged sword, it penetrates even to dividing soul and spirit, joints and marrow; it judges the thoughts and attitudes of the heart."
-   Hebrews 4:12

Lifeguard's Pole & Hook

Lifeguards have a tool to help with the rescue of struggling swimmers. It's a pole with a hook.

We do the right thing, but we always seem to mess up. We get caught up in our mistakes. We struggle in the water and are unable to save ourselves. We need to be rescued.

When you can't make things right … when there is nothing else to do … when you hit rock bottom … when you have done all you can and it still isn't enough … it's okay. It's all part of God's plan.

It's not about what you can do. It's about what Jesus has done. He is our lifeguard. His cross is reaching out like a lifeguard's pole & hook. All you have to do is grab it. It is enough to hold on to the cross when there is nothing else. Jesus's death and resurrection rescues us. His death is enough when nothing else is. The cross is your salvation. Reach out and grab hold of it.

"For it is by grace you have been saved, through faith—and this is not from yourselves, it is the gift of God—not by works, so that no one can boast." – Ephesians 2:8-9

The White Rose

One simple white rose lay in the sand along my path. It couldn't have been there long. It hadn't started to wilt yet. But there it laid as if meant for me.

Some gifts are so special. Maybe it's because they are exactly what we wanted or maybe it's because they are exactly what we needed. Maybe it's because of the thought that went into it or maybe because of the tender love shown by the giver.

I have this silly notion on my walks that the flowers growing along my way were placed there especially for me by a God who loves me. Imagine my surprise to find a beautiful, perfectly cut rose in my path along Weko Beach. It could have been left by anyone, but I choose to believe it was one of those special gifts God left behind for me— special because of the tender love I know He has for me.

God's love for you is real. It is eternal. He shows it in the small gestures like a white rose left on the beach for you to find.

"I have loved you with an everlasting love."
— Jeremiah 31:3

Different Boards

Wood used for a step is different than wood used for a railing. It takes thicker and bigger boards to create a solid foundation. The wood is different but they come together to form the boardwalk.

God offers help for each situation. We may need a big, thick board to deal with the major issues of life or we may need a railing to steady ourselves. Maybe we need the next board to step on. Whatever it is, God's got us covered.

From my own personal experience, I have found that hanging onto a Bible verse helped for a time. Another verse helped for yet another time. Just as there are different boards for different purposes, there are different Bible verses for each situation you face.

Whatever you are going through, find a Bible verse for your situation and focus on it.

"All scripture is God-breathed and is useful ... so that the servant of God may be thoroughly equipped for every good work."
– 2 Timothy 3:16-17

The Beach Brat

His temper tantrum caught the attention of everyone on the beach. All I could hear was his crying and screaming. He didn't know any better—he was too young.

Haven't we all experienced wrong at the hand of our fellow church goers? Maybe it's something so small as a flippant remark or so big as breaking a commandment. People mess up and we react in different ways. Some shrug it off while others can't get past it.

You probably have experienced this. I did at a relatively early age and I'm thankful for the lesson I learned. Why turn away from God when it is people that are messing up? It's not Him. He is still perfect, loving, and just. It's like refusing to go to the beach ever again because of one bratty kid. The beach isn't responsible for that. So when a fellow church goer messes up, remember it was the person that was responsible and not God.

Don't turn your back on God. He is not the beach brat.

"The righteousness of the righteous will be credited to them, and the wickedness of the wicked will be charged against them."
– Ezekiel 18:20

The Sun Shines

The sun had risen but I couldn't see it yet along Weko Beach. The trees and the dunes blocked its rays from actually shining onto the beach where I was.

When change is in the air and we struggle with it, it's easy to be afraid. We see the changing circumstances and they far out-weigh our abilities. We start thinking hope is for everyone but us. It's like watching the sun shine on everyone else, while we walk along in the dark.

You may feel unworthy of God's help. Maybe you haven't been "Christian" enough. Maybe you messed up badly or maybe you don't believe in God. God will strengthen you regardless. Not because of what you have or haven't done, but because of who He is. His help will show you and others He is God.

The sun will shine on you too. Hope in God.

"I will strengthen you, though you have not acknowledged Me, so that from the rising of the sun to the place of its setting people may know there is none besides Me. I am the Lord."
– Isaiah 45:5-6

Thankful Hand

I watched as the waves rolled back into Lake Michigan. It left behind sand. It got me thinking how God is the giver of life. He deals the hand we get, determining our days and how those days go, just as Lake Michigan determines how much sand to leave on the beach.

Stop and think about your life—the good and the bad. Aren't you thankful for it? Sure, maybe things didn't happen exactly as you hoped, but look at it and see what God has done through everything. Either He blessed you more than what your expected or He didn't. Those times in my life when God didn't meet my expectations turned out to be the times I grew closer to Him, trusting and actively learning what faith meant. I may not have gotten my expectations, but I did get something more valuable—faith born out of my experiences—experiences I can look back on now to reassure me of His goodness and His power. Those are things you may not often pray for even though you may need them more than the expectations you do pray for.

Be thankful for the hand God has dealt you.

"For with You is the fountain of life; in Your light we see light." – Psalm 36:9

Beach Glass Doesn't Cut

The young boy asked, "Do people collect beach glass so others don't cut their feet on it when they walk on the beach?" He didn't understand that beach glass isn't sharp when refined by the water.

Some people misunderstand God and His Word. They don't see Him as a blessing, but as something cutting into their life interfering with their goals and what they want. They see God the same way that young boy saw beach glass. Not as a blessing but as something sharp and dangerous.

How do you see God? Do you see the good only He can bring? Or do you see Him as a harsh, distant God who doesn't care about your hurts and pain? He is not sharp. He cares. He gives you His Word so you don't cut your feet as you walk through life.

"Blessed is the one who does not walk in step with the wicked or stand in the way that sinners take or sit in the company of mockers, but whose delight is in the law of the Lord, and who meditates on His law day and night."
– Psalms 1:1-2

The Helicopter

I stopped what I was doing. When I heard the engine and saw the helicopter heading south along the beach, it wasn't hard to figure out there was trouble somewhere. The waters were rough today and not the safest.

Trouble can hit anytime and anywhere. None of us are immune to it and, when it happens to us, we want all the help we can get.

I quietly said a silent prayer as I watched the helicopter disappear out of sight. I didn't know what the situation was or who was involved. If it were me I would want all the help I could get. I would want the prayers of people like you to bring God's hand into the situation. You don't have to know who to pray for or what to pray. They don't even have to know you are praying for them, and they may not even want your prayers ...

But pray.

"Brothers and sisters, pray for us."
— 1 Thessalonians 5:25

Tiny Treasures

My kids ran ahead of me, leaving their tiny footprints in the wet sand. I watched them, knowing someday I wouldn't see those tiny prints. My kids would grow up, and something in this mother's heart stirred.

What is more precious to a parent than their children? Little do we understand that having children changes life. What was once important to us takes a backseat. I don't think we can ever fully comprehend that until we actually have children of our own. How precious they are to our lives.

How precious you are to your Father in heaven too! He blesses you with family and what they bring into your life. That day on the beach, my heart stirred realizing how precious those moments with my children are. God used their tiny footprints in the wet sand to remind me of what's really important. It's not success, material possessions, image … it's about the love you share with your kids in the precious moments called life.

Treasure those tiny footprints.

"Children are a heritage from the Lord, offspring a reward from Him." – Psalm 127:3

Living Stones

Stones are not my thing. I don't collect them. I have no interest in them. They serve no purpose. I am glad I am a living human being instead of a stone.

Who would want to be a stone? We sit on the beach in all kinds of weather with nothing to do. We would be hard and cold. Not something any of us would aspire for our lives.

It's interesting that the Bible mentions people becoming living stones. By living, it makes me think of a stone other than cold and hard. When you are filled with the Holy Spirit, your cold, hard heart changes to become more like Christ's. You become a living stone able to house the Holy Spirit—a livable house for God.

Aspire to be a living stone. Invite the Holy Spirit in.

"You also, like living stones, are being built into a spiritual house." – 1 Peter 2:5

A Log Has Been Placed

I am usually glad to see a log placed across the creek on my walks at Weko Beach. It means I can walk farther if I want to. Some days there is a log and other days there isn't. On a cold day when there isn't a log, I have to find a different way over the creek or that's the end of my walk.

There are days and circumstances when we can't see how to move forward. We look for answers but they don't come. We look for a way out and there is none. It's like walking up to the creek on Weko Beach and not seeing a way past it.

When you come up against a wall, when you have no answers, when you have nothing left within to make things work … God has a way. If He can move the Red Sea to make a way for the Israelites, He can make a way for you. If He can make a way for human kind and animals to survive a world-wide flood, He can make a way for you. If He can make a way for sinners to get to Heaven, He can make a way for you.

God is into placing logs across the creeks in life.

"I am making a way in the wilderness and streams in the wasteland." – Isaiah 43:19

Picking Up My Trash

At the end of a day on the beach, I pick up my trash. It either ends up in the waste basket on the way to the car or it gets stuck in a bag to be cleaned out later at home.

Guilt. It's hard to clean up. It hangs there with each simple reminder of the mistakes we've made and want to forget. We try to make things right again, but no matter how hard we try, the slate never seems clean. It's like going to Weko Beach and leaving some trash behind after trying to clean up.

Like you, I try to clean my messes up. I apologize or change what I did wrong, but it's not enough. I can't take back what I've done. Go to God every time the guilt creeps back in and pray about it. Prayers not only admit the wrong. They can include Scripture reassuring you of your forgiveness.

Let the guilt go. God cleans up your trash.

"Let us draw near to God ... with the full assurance that faith brings, having our hearts sprinkled to cleanse us from a guilty conscience."
– Hebrews 10:22

Replacements

The new boards looked out of place on the boardwalk. They weren't weathered and old like the rest. Their newness shouted out their "in-ness" over the "so-out-of-it" weathered boards.

Life has a way of dating things. Fads come and go. Each generation tells us their way is better because of the advances in technology and gains in scientific discoveries. It's like they scream out their "in-ness." What was from long ago is now "so-out-of-it."

Jesus never changes. He is the same throughout the ages. He is the only way to the Father. No matter what advances are made, nothing will replace Him. He is the truth, and truth never changes.

When you build your foundation by the choices you make, build it on what never changes—the Truth.

"Jesus Christ is the same yesterday and today and forever." – Hebrews 13:8

Golden Grass

The season was changing at Weko Beach. The air was getting cooler. The crowds were thinning out. The leaves were turning colors. Fall was here. The green beach grass even turned a shade of gold.

One of the inevitable changes in life is our age. We can't stop it as much as some of us may want to. It comes as the fall comes, turning the grass a golden color. Our wrinkles and bags set in along with the gray hair.

You may be one of those people fighting the aging process. The "golden" years don't seem so golden to you. Maybe the "golden" is not in wealth or health or age or peaceful times. Maybe it is inside—an inner confidence and strength brought on by years learning Who to turn to and Who to trust and Who to place your hope in. You no longer need the strength of your youth when you have a lifetime of experience leaning on Jesus and building a relationship with Him

Enjoy the golden years with Him.

"The glory of young men is their strength; gray hair is the splendor of the old."
— Proverb 20:29

Stand Still

I love the waves. I loved swimming in them as a child. Back then, I didn't know to be afraid of big waves or bad swimming conditions.

We can see things coming at us … situations we don't know how to handle. We see them roaring at us like a big, unstoppable wave. We find ourselves standing there, frozen in place, watching as it comes.

When situations bigger than you rush towards you, all you can do is stand there. You can't stop it. Maybe you don't know how to stop it or maybe it's out of your control. It is so comforting and encouraging knowing God is way bigger than the situations you face. He is more powerful than the big waves of anxiety, grief, worry, and fear. In those times, God's purpose may be for you to stand still and watch as He deals with the big waves coming at you. God may want you to see what *He* can do and how much more *He* is than the waves coming at you.

Stand still and watch what God can do.

"You rule over the surging sea; when its waves mount up, You still them." – Psalm 89:9

A Beautiful Mess

I was complaining again. Sand all over the inside of my car, sand on the floors at home. It's the downside of going to the beach. My picture-perfect idea of a fun and loving family day at the beach ended up not so picture-perfect. What a mess.

We don't like days that aren't picture-perfect. They can be downright ugly. All our planning to make things perfect fall short and we are left with a mess like my failed picture-perfect family day at the beach.

God allows both picture-perfect days and messy days. His plans don't always include a beautiful day for you. Sometimes He wants you to experience messy days so the beauty of it can shine through. There is nothing more beautiful than people honoring God on a messy day. It brings joy to the surface that, yes, God is real, and our hope is renewed.

Bring the beauty into your messy days.

"Call on Me in the day of trouble; I will deliver you, and you will honor Me." – Psalm 50:15

Unique Stones

If stones are unique, they pop. This one was very different. It almost had a plaid look to it. It stood out from the dull, boring stones. I have seen a few other unique stones—a green one and, of course, those bright, translucent white stones.

Sometimes we want to be different. We want to stand out in the crowd and be noticed. We want to be recognized for our talents. Others are happy taking a back seat, being one of those boring and dull people. We don't stand out in the crowd. Our accomplishments and what we do go by unnoticed and it's okay. We like it that way.

Whichever way you fall, you are a unique and talented person with a different set of abilities, attitudes, and features. It's not a bad thing but a good thing. It is exactly what God made you to be.

Make the most of who you are whether you are a stone that pops or one lost among the rest.

"You knit me together in my mother's womb. I am fearfully and wonderfully made."
— Psalms 139:13-14

Love the Beach

Disappointed, I headed to the beach. I realized then the choice I would have to make: go to the beach alone or don't go at all.

The problem with people who don't go to the beach is they don't care enough about the beach. They are less likely to encourage you to go. The more you hang around them, the more chance you won't go to the beach either. People who love the beach will jump at the opportunity and are more likely to encourage you to go too.

Not all of us are blessed with a spouse, children, extended family, or friends who love God. It forces us to choose to go to church alone or not go at all.

If you find yourself in that situation, be aware of their lack of commitment and how it can influence you to cut corners or skip out on fellowship. The good news is, you can remain committed and go alone.

Go to the Beach alone if you have to, but go.

"Bad company corrupts good character."
− 1 Corinthians 15:33

A Washed-Up Table

It was out-of-place—a picnic table washed up on the shores of Lake Michigan. Not where it should have been. Although it was half-buried in the sand, it provided a nice resting spot for a worn-out beachgoer.

Life can make us feel washed up. People say things or do things to make us feel like, really, nothing. Maybe they don't even say anything. Maybe they just ignore us as if we aren't worth the time or effort.

On those days when you'd rather stay inside and hide from others, remember the Lord. He knows who is giving you a hard time and who is making your life difficult. Only He can give you victory to overcome what others put in front of you. It doesn't matter what it is or where it is, God has what you need to overcome.

Anticipate and celebrate your victories as you sit at the table God has washed up on the shores of your life.

"You prepare a table before me in the presence of my enemies." – Psalm 23:5

Wood Knots

No matter where I walked on the boardwalk, they were there—knots in the wood. Some may think they are ugly, but not me. I think they add character to the wood.

We want perfection—wood without knots. Life isn't like that though. Every life comes with its knots. They come from past hurts and failures. They stamp our lives with scars, constantly reminding us of them. We want to hide them and pretend they don't exist, but they happened. We can't go back in time to change them.

You can learn to love your scars. Just like the wood knots add character to the boardwalk, your scars add character to who you are. They no longer have to be ugly reminders of past hurts and failures. When you call on God to heal them, He shows you the beauty of your character that developed from those hurts and failures. Your scars become reminders of life-changing decisions you made and of situations you have overcome.

Love the character that knots bring.

"Lord my God, I called to You for help, and You healed me." – Psalm 30:2

Throw off the Leash

The friendly dog walked past me wagging his tail. He was well-behaved. He didn't jump. He didn't bark. I wondered how he would do if unleashed. I could imagine him joyfully running (or walking) alongside his owners taking in the whole beach thing.

There are many things holding us back, from bad habits to poor judgement. We are like a dog on a leash. We want to be free to enjoy life and all that is waiting for us, but mistakes, bad habits, and poor judgement keep us tied up.

It's not until you look at yourself that you can start moving ahead. Admit your faults. The admitting can unleash whatever is holding on to you. Then get rid of it.

Throw off the leash and joyfully run along life with your Owner.

"Let us throw off everything that hinders and the sin that so easily entangles. And let us run with perseverance the race marked out for us."
— Hebrews 12:1

TV

I laid there on the beach with my friends soaking up the sun. At sixteen, it didn't bother me at all that the local television station was there filming Weko Beach for a segment announcing the start of summer.

Changes may come unannounced. Many of us like to prepare so that when something happens it doesn't get us in an uproar. We like those segments on TV announcing the change of seasons. It leaves us feeling in control.

What about you? How do you handle unexpected changes? Jesus is coming back. Things are going to change *and* it will be unannounced. Will He find you laying on the beach soaking in the rays trying to get the most out of this life or will He find you standing in the Water trying to draw close to Him?

"About times and dates we do not need to write to you, for you know very well that the day of the Lord will come like a thief in the night."
– 1 Thessalonians 5:1-2

September

"The paths don't matter as much as the Water
they lead to."

White Waters

The water was anything but calm. As it turned over with each crash of a wave, it turned white—almost foamy.

Have you ever looked at the things you've done wrong in your life? I remember seeing how I chose to handle certain situations and realizing how wrong I really was. I didn't like what I saw. It hurt.

Jesus is like those waves on the beach. He comes over you and turns you white. He cleanses the wrong choices you made and makes you clean. He did that through His death on the cross, and you know the nice thing about it? He died while you were still doing things wrong. The whole reason for His death was to wash over your mistakes, your faults, your failures, whatever you want to call it. He makes you white—like foamy water—in God's eyes.

And ... the waves keep coming.

"Wash me and I shall be whiter than snow."
— Psalm 51:7

Aging Eyes

I held up my hand and squinted at it. I could barely make it out, but my daughter was right. It was probably the smallest Indian bead I had ever seen. It was like one small grain of sand. I was amazed she even noticed it. I had grown accustomed to the idea that I would not be able to find every Indian bead, especially the harder-to-see smaller ones. I saw the power of a young child's vision.

Children have a way of seeing the blessings we miss. Maybe it's because they are seeing it for the first time. Or maybe it's because their vision is better. As time goes along we get accustom to life as we see it, and we stop looking closely at things, thinking we have seen it all, but sometimes by doing that we miss the little blessings of life.

Pray to God to open your eyes to the wonderful blessings He has for you, for ...

Aging eyes with child-like vision.

"Open my eyes that I may see wonderful things in Your law." — Psalm 119:18

Sandals

I ran looking for shade wherever I could find it. It got so bad I threw my towel down halfway to the water and stood on it for a minute or two. The sand was hot—really hot. If I had my sandals on, I wouldn't have burned my feet.

Do we do anything to prepare ahead of time for potential problems? Most of us are just happy not to have them. We consider it a break and take the time to enjoy life as it is until things happen and we find ourselves unprepared.

Life will not always be carefree and easy. God says so in His Word. You will have problems. Temptations will come, but God also says to be prepared. Read, study, and meditate on His Word. That's putting on the armor and being prepared.

The time to put on your sandals is now before you hit the hot sand.

"Put on the full armor of God, so that you can take your stand against the devil's schemes."
– Ephesians 6:11

Look Back on the Moments

A young girl on the beach surrounded by photography equipment was obviously having her senior pictures taken. Other times it has been a wedding party. They are there to remember the moment years down the road.

We all have special moments in our lives marking the beginning of something new or maybe even the end, signifying a major accomplishment. We have other significant moments impacting our lives. Not everyone gets caught in a photo, but they do get caught in your memories.

Good or bad - inspiration, confidence, and encouragement can be drawn from remembering those moments. When you remember what God has done in the past or even what He has done in the Bible, it can keep you hanging in there to face the struggles that glare at you today. It gives hope and a different outlook.

Look back at the captured moments of what God has done.

"I will remember the deeds of the Lord; yes, I will remember Your miracles of long ago."
– Psalm 77:11

Just a Small Stone

These were just small, useless stones. I looked at them as I searched for some Indian beads. It reminded me of how I had been feeling lately ... small and useless, like I had nothing to offer.

Haven't we all compared ourselves to family, friends, and others and come up short? We feel like we are a small, useless stone on the beach. It's not fun and it really doesn't help anyone.

The Bible tells you to look at your own actions and test them. It doesn't say anything about comparing them to others. Impossible expectations happen when you set goals based on someone else's abilities. A good confidence builder sets a goal based on your own abilities, not someone else's.

Think about it. Small stones are useful too.

"Each one should test their own actions. Then they can take pride in themselves alone, without comparing themselves to someone else."
- Galatians 6:4

Singing Crickets

The crickets' song hung in the evening air as I walked along the beach. Their song sounded so happy and full of joy. It made me want to sing out with them.

We go through difficult things—sometimes over and over again. It can crush our spirits and cause us to lose the songs in our lives.

As I listened to the crickets sing, it made me think of all God has brought me through—the good times and overcoming the bad times. I have a lot to be thankful for. I have a lot to sing about. The more you focus on what God has blessed you with and the more you focus on how He has worked out your tough situations, the more the song grows. You can't help but have a song inside when you focus on Him.

Sing with the crickets for all God has done!

"Let the heavens rejoice, let the earth be glad; let the sea resound, and all that is in it. Let the fields be jubilant, and everything in them; let all the trees of the forest sing for joy."
– Psalms 96:11-12

Sights from on High

I climbed the boardwalk at Weko Beach. Along the way I stopped a few times to look out over everything. When I reached the top, it was a sight for sore eyes.

Our calling takes us to new levels. We learn and understand new things. We experience new things as we climb. There are new sights—sights that amaze us.

Have you ever questioned following your life calling? Take a walk on the boardwalk. Pause a few times and be amazed at the sights. When you follow what you believe God has called you to, you are giving Him the opportunity to show you new sights from on high. You are giving God the opportunity to show Himself and His works. God can bless you when you follow your calling. Be joyful. Be amazed at what you see Him do along the way.

Sights for sore eyes come from above.

"But blessed are your eyes because they see."
— Matthew 13:16

Pack Up the Umbrella

I had to laugh. It was comical sitting on Weko Beach watching the beachgoers. The wind would pick up their planted umbrellas, and on to their feet the beachgoers jumped chasing it down. They finally gave up and left the umbrellas down.

Sometimes I make the mistake thinking I can change things by what I do. Oh, I know in my head God is all-powerful and sovereign, but I'm not always willing to accept His plans. I keep going back in my meager little efforts to change what He may have in mind for me. It's like those beachgoers going back and replanting an umbrella hoping it will stand in the face of a strong, powerful wind sent by God. Human efforts cannot change what God has planned.

Pack up the umbrella. It's not going to stand against God's winds.

"For the Lord Almighty has purposed, and who can thwart Him? His hand is stretched out, and who can turn it back?" – Isaiah 14:27

Rainy Day Plans

The weather had changed quickly as I hurried back to my car. The rain started to fall, and I could see in the distance other beachgoers scrambling to pack up and run for safety. The calm water was now rippled with raindrops.

None of us go through life doing everything right. No one goes through life without scars from past choices, whether our own or others'. All that is wrong in our lives is because of sin.

God sends change. He decided to change things in Noah's time so He started the rain. Why? To get rid of the sin so prevalent at the time. The rain on the beach changed my plans. You don't have to worry about another world-wide flood, but God can still send the rain at any time to change your plans. The question is: Are you living life Noah's way or the rest of the world's way?

What happens to you in the rain will tell.

"Seven days from now I will send rain on the earth for forty days and forty nights, and I will wipe from the face of the earth every living creature I have made." – Genesis 7:4

Watermarked

You can tell when something has been in the water for a while. Driftwood has almost a spongy kind of look to it that regular wood doesn't have. Beach glass has smooth edges while broken glass has sharp ones. Even the stones can have markings. They all have one thing in common. They have been touched by the water.

I am tempted at times to carry the shame of the circumstances of my life—circumstances I'm not proud of, circumstances I never asked for. They make me feel different from others. They make me feel broken and inferior.

When I focus on what God has done for and through me in those circumstances, I don't have to be ashamed. I am different because God has touched me through them just as a piece of driftwood is different because it has been touched by water. The circumstances you carry can be a reminder of times when God has touched you and left His mark.

You have been watermarked by God.

"God set His seal of ownership on us and put His Spirit in our hearts." – 2 Corinthians 1:21-22

Smirnoff Bottle

Sure, I was collecting beach glass, but that's not what I really had in mind. A small Smirnoff bottle lay in the grass along the beach. Someone emptied its contents and threw it down.

We perceive things differently. There probably isn't one person in this world who perceives everything the same as you do. The person who drank the Smirnoff saw the drink as a blessing and the bottle as trash. I saw it differently. Someday that Smirnoff bottle is going to end up in Lake Michigan and become beach glass that someone will pick up and add to their collection.

Growth in our relationship with God comes in the form of changed values. What was considered a blessing before is not one now. We are changed from valuing the drink to valuing the bottle.

"I consider everything a loss because of the surpassing worth of knowing Christ Jesus my Lord." – Philippians 3:8

Rolling Down the Dunes

The parents stood at the top watching their kids roll down the sand dune like a log, laughing and squealing until they reached the bottom.

It's easier to go with the flow. We don't ruffle any feathers and there's less chance we will find ourselves on the outs if we roll along with the crowd.

The problem with rolling through life is that it's like rolling down a sand dune. It only heads in one direction— down. At some point along the way you have to take a stand. If you don't, you will end up at the bottom having to climb your way back up.

God loves the things in life that bring good. He loves justice. He loves righteousness. When you roll with the flow through life, it's very likely justice and righteousness are being ignored and good things are being missed. When justice and righteousness aren't happening, God's will is not happening either.

Don't roll down the dune. Take your stand.

"But let justice roll on like a river, righteousness like a never-failing stream." – Amos 5:24

Flips

My sisters and my brother would get excited when Dad came out into the water with us. He lifted us up and flipped us back into the water. As I grew, my friends and I took turns cuffing our hands together to form a foothold for each other to stand up on and flip off of. We were always careful not to flip where anyone could get hurt.

People can be a good or bad influence. They can set you on the right path or drag you on a downward spiral.

Who are the people you hang with? Do they send you in the right direction? Those who care about you care enough about the outcome of your decisions. They care about what your decisions bring into your life. They care about building you up and sending you off in a positive direction.

A good friend flips you into the right direction ... into the Water.

"Therefore encourage one another and build each other up, just as in fact you are doing."
– 1 Thessalonians 5:11

Skipping It Back

The stone was in the shallow water, and it was perfect for skipping. I picked it up and walked out of the water. Positioning the stone just right, I flicked it out and watched as it skipped back over the water until it disappeared.

We tend to think the abilities we have are ours. They are ours to do with as we please. We may have worked hard to develop them. We may have practiced and studied and put in tons of time to have that skill or knowledge. Our blood, sweat, and tears seem to cement the idea that WE are the ones responsible for our talents and WE have the right to decide how we use them.

What seems to get missed is that God allows you the time, the growth, the understanding, the drive, and the opportunities to develop your talents. Knowing that can make you think twice about how to use them. God still allows you to make the choice though.

Will you skip your stone back out to the Water?

"We have given You only what comes from Your hand." – 1 Chronicles 29:14

Empty Stomachs

They flew over the water with ease, steadfastly gliding across Lake Michigan hunting for food. Occasionally a sea gull dipped into the water to catch a fish. They were searching for food to fill their empty stomachs.

We feel empty inside. We search for fulfillment. We try to fill the emptiness with busyness, with goals, with possessions. It's unending—a steadfast effort—trying to fill what is missing. We may find temporary fulfillment, but it never seems to last.

I watched the sea gulls fly about a foot above the water. They knew instinctively where to go and they kept coming back. God provided you and I with Jesus. He is our spiritual food. He is the lasting, eternal fulfillment missing in an empty life. He doesn't take away the problems but He gives purpose. He eliminates the emptiness and gives hope.

Jesus fills your emptiness with life.

"For the bread of God is the bread that comes down from heaven and gives life to the world. I am the bread of life." – John 6:33-35

Cross Roads

I found myself at a crossroad near the top of the boardwalk. Which way do I go?

Things can easily get confusing if we don't know what to do … if we have options. We worry we will make the wrong choice, and we struggle with knowing what the right choice is.

I made my choice to go one direction as I stood at the crossroad on the boardwalk. It didn't really even matter. My goal was to walk the boardwalk. Following God is your main calling in life. All else will fall into place. When faced with choices taking you in different directions, you don't have to worry. The Bible tells you when you focus on God that whatever direction you take, you prosper. Maybe it's not so much about the decisions you make as much as it is about what God can do.

Trust in God at the crossroads.

*"… whose delight is in the law of the Lord, and
who meditates on His law day and night....
Whatever they do prospers."*
– Psalms 1:2-3

Prepare

As a teenager I was in such a hurry to get to the beach that I didn't waste any time packing enough snacks or water. Now I sat there wishing I had prepared better. I was starving, and I ran out of water.

It's important to be prepared. We start learning that at a young age. During the school years, we learn to read our assignments and to complete our homework on time or suffer the consequences. As adults we learn the importance of paying our bills on time and getting to work on time. We learn the importance of being prepared when we are sitting on a beach blanket starving and thirsty.

But what about being prepared spiritually? Being ready for Jesus to come back? Being ready for the next situation satan throws at us? If we take the time and effort to prepare for school, work, and life in general, can't we prepare ourselves for times of temptation too? For eternity? We prepare by reading the Bible today—not tomorrow.

"The foolish ones took their lamps but did not take any oil with them. ... Therefore keep watch, because you do not know the day or the hour." – Matthew 25:3, 13

Bulldozed

The weather takes its toll on Weko Beach each year. Fences are put up along the sand to protect the beach from the winter winds. Some years in early spring there are bulldozers called in to restore the beach.

Some things never change while others change our lives forever. Some changes leave us feeling broken. We don't know how to fix things.

When you feel broken and you have no idea how to fix things, there is the one and only God who knows. He knows and understands your brokenness and how to fix it. You are not without hope. When you are broken, God is not. When you don't understand, God does. He loves and cares for you and, in His wonderful timing and way, He restores you just like a bulldozer restoring the beach.

Hope in God's bulldozing.

"He refreshes my soul." – Psalm 23:3

Step into the Water

Summer days in Michigan can be downright hot—too hot when a person doesn't want to do anything but sit in the shade for relief from the heat. I found myself on Weko Beach on one of those days. I stepped into the water, and it felt so refreshing on such a hot muggy day.

On days when life gets to be too much, when it stifles you and all you can do is nothing—you need a break. You need time to step back and refresh yourself. Just like Lake Michigan refreshing on a hot muggy day, God is able to refresh the tired and weary person. When things start wearing on you, when you feel tired and weary, get your Bible out; sing some songs of praise; find a quiet place of solitude and talk to God.

Step into the Water and be refreshed.

"I will refresh the weary and satisfy the faint."
— Jeremiah 31:25

Indian Bead in the Making

There it laid on the beach … a big dead fish. *There are going to be some big Indian beads from that fish someday, I thought to myself. Wouldn't it be nice if I could just grab those beads right now!*

Instant gratification—getting what we want now.

Patience, though, can be a long wait. We try to make things happen when maybe we shouldn't. I could have tried to get the Indian beads from the dead fish laying on the beach but I would have had to go through the dead fish only to find bones still intact. It needed to be worked over by the water.

God has blessings for you but maybe right now is not the time. Maybe it's still in the making like fish bones needing the touch of water.

Be patient. Some blessings are still in the making.

"Wait for the Lord; be strong and take heart and Wait for the Lord." – Psalm 27:14

A Handful

I saw them walking down the beach. I could tell it was a struggle. The dog yanked and pulled at the leash whenever beachgoers passed by. The owner held onto the leash with a strong, steady hold. "That's a friendly dog!" I said as they came near me. "He's a handful," they replied.

Some of our relationships can be like that. A struggle. A tug here and a pull there. With each passing situation, we can be at odds with that difficult person in our lives.

I have a few in my life that I have tried to change, to teach them a better way. It never worked and usually ended badly. God calls us to love them, not to change them. That's His job. Find the good in them and love them for that. And if that fails … love them because it is an opportunity for a heavenly reward.

Love your handfuls and be rewarded.

"For if you love those who love you, what reward will you get?" – Matthew 5:46

Different Paths

At the end of the boardwalk are steps down to the sand. These steps give way to different paths through the grassy hills leading to Lake Michigan.

Don't we sometimes judge people's true "Christianity" based on their past or on the church they go to or on the things they are or are not involved in now.

God's ways are not our ways. He has innumerable ways of doing things, of bringing people close to Him, of representing Himself to the world. He can draw someone close to Him by the blessings He pours out while drawing others by the pain and suffering. Pouring out blessings may work better on some, while pain and suffering may work better for others.

Don't judge others because of the path they came to know Jesus. The point is they are here with us. Each of us have taken a different path to get to where we are with Jesus. The paths don't matter as much as the Water they lead to.

"Show me Your ways, Lord, teach me Your paths." – Psalm 25:4

Teamwork

I walked along Weko Beach stepping carefully on the small pebbles and stones gathered along the water. I wasn't really enjoying myself. Up ahead, there were only a few pebbles and stones scattered here and there. That's where I wanted to be.

Teamwork. I hear about it every so often. I perk up a little and listen to who is saying what about it. Why? I don't consider myself a big team player. Sure, I'll help someone out if they need help. If I'm asked to do something, I have no problem saying yes. But give me instructions and set the goals, and I'm off and running on whatever project. I actually prefer working alone over working in a team. I have heard so many times about the importance of teamwork that I feel guilty knowing I like working and doing things on my own.

My thoughts on teamwork are different from the majority. You may be different in other ways. Embrace it. God made you that way. Some of us prefer scarce pebbles and stones. It's part of the team makeup.

"Just as a body, though one, has many parts, but all its many parts form one body, so it is with Christ." – 1 Corinthians 12:12

Red Flags

On days when water conditions are dangerous, Weko Beach hangs red flags as warning signs. These flags are meant to save lives.

We don't always want to live the way God wants us to. If we are honest with ourselves, God seems to rain on our parade, taking all the fun out of life. For some, it is reason enough to turn away from Him.

It's easy to look at the rough waves of Lake Michigan and understand why the red flags are out. The flags are there to protect and save lives. God's ways are there to protect and save lives too. Life will have its problems, but His ways are there to walk you through them without losing it. His ways are there to save your life from drowning in problems too big to handle. His ways are not meant to take the fun out of life, but to protect and save it.

The ways of God are His red flags to protect and save life.

"The thief comes only to steal and kill and destroy; I have come that they may have life and have it to the full." – John 10:10

Flowing Streams

It was beautiful. The fall colors, the boardwalk I stood on, the stream flowing underneath the boardwalk. I looked over the rail. The stream spewed out from under the boardwalk as if it came from the boardwalk itself.

Our foremost calling in life is to follow God. We have days when we believe we hit the mark. Other days, we wonder. We can't seem to see the difference we make in following Him and we start to question if we really are living life for God. Shouldn't He be spewing out from us so there is no question in our minds or anyone else's?

I've been there. I've questioned my own Christian walk. I've wondered if I was really living for God. I want to spew out Christ in me just like a stream rushing out from under the boardwalk. I've had many days where I missed the mark. I'm not alone.

What about you? How do you handle it when you miss the mark? Simple. Believe that Jesus is Lord. It's not based on you getting it right. Believe and let the water flow.

"Whoever believes in Me ... rivers of living water will flow from within them." – John 7:38

Kids on the Boardwalk

I remember the day we took our daughter for a walk on the boardwalk for the first time. She was bundled up in her small winter coat and boots. It was a cold, wintery day, but she still was able to see the lake and the beach from the heights.

Our children are important to us. As parents we want to pass along our values and enable them to carve out a good life through the choices they make.

How can you do that? It's done by living out what is important to you. If God is important to you, let them see it. Let them see and be a part of how you connect with Him. Let them be a part of what He has called you to do with your life. Talk to them about it so they know and understand why you do what you do. It teaches them.

Take your kids for a walk on the boardwalk.

"Impress them on your children. Talk about them when you sit at home and when you walk along the road, when you lie down and when you get up." – Deuteronomy 6:7

Clouds or No Clouds

There were not a lot of people on the beach. I too considered not coming. The sky was overcast and there were a lot of clouds. It looked as if it could rain any moment. That was what kept most beachgoers home today.

Problems have a way of getting the best of us. They bother and upset us so much that all we can do is focus on them. We hide away in our homes as if our problems won't find us there, much like staying home from the beach on a cloudy, overcast day.

Your problems can be distracting, and you can't hide from them. Most will stay where they are until dealt with. You don't have to worry or get upset by what's on your plate. Go first to God. Listen and learn what He has to say. He has a way of taking the pressure off. That is the one thing needed.

Clouds or no clouds, sit at the Lord's feet.

"She had a sister named Mary, who sat at the Lord's feet listening to what He said. But Martha was distracted by all the preparations that had to be made."—Luke 10:39-40

Sandals Off

When we go to the beach, we take our sandals off before going into the water. It's perfectly fitting to go barefoot at the beach. Go to any other public place and shoes are required, but not here.

I am reminded of Moses when he saw the burning bush. God told him to take his shoes off because he was standing on holy ground. This wasn't the only time in the Bible that we read of shoes coming off because of holy ground. It's a lot like taking our sandals off to go in to the water.

Most places treat bare feet as a disrespectful act, but God sees it as an act of respect. When you approach God, it is a holy moment because He is holy. I don't know about you, but I want to come as close as I can get to His holiness. I don't want my sandals standing in the way.

Show some respect. Take off your sandals.

"Then the Lord said to him, Take off your sandals, for the place you are standing is holy ground."
– Acts 7:33

Swoop In

They flocked to the people throwing bread crumbs in the air. In a smooth swoop one sea gull flew by and swept up the tossed bread. Others ate it up before it hit the ground. It was their source of food and they eagerly grabbed every crumb available.

God provides us living bread straight from heaven—His Word. We normally think food is what sustains us, but the Bible clearly tells us we cannot live life with food alone. We need His Word to guide and help us.

Are you eager to grab the Word of God? Is it the source of your life? Going to church, reading the Word, listening to Christian music—these are ways we grab on to God's Bread of Life.

Swoop in and eagerly grab the Bread from heaven.

"For the bread of God is the bread that comes down from heaven and gives life to the world."
– John 6:33

Pass on the Love

From a very young age, I grew up loving the beach and I still do. I brought my kids to Weko Beach. We dug in the sand and played in the water. We took walks along the lake and simply enjoyed life on the beach.

We all have things we love, things we want to pass on to our children, things we want to experience with them. One of mine was summers on Lake Michigan.

You pass along your love of things to your children by letting them experience it with you. Those days on Weko Beach passed on my love of the beach to my kids. I see my love for the beach and the outdoors especially in my son. He goes for walks and when he feels a need to get out for a while, that is usually where he is headed.

Do you love God enough to choose experiences that bring you closer to Him? Include your kids. It's an opportunity to let His love pass on to them.

"Start children off on the way they should go, and even when they are old they will not turn from it." – Proverb 22:6

October

"Dependable, endless Water."

A Connection

I looked across the water and saw Gary. Bridgman, Michigan and Gary, Indiana have something in common … Lake Michigan. I felt a sense of connection to the people there.

Have you ever listened to the news? Everything speaks of doom and gloom. We easily walk away wondering what is wrong with people. We can't relate to others or their situations. Maybe because they are so different from our own experiences and beliefs. We can't connect.

God tells you to put on love which can bind people together perfectly. Just as Lake Michigan gives a sense of connection to the people across the lake, God can give a sense of connection through His love. When you look at others through the eyes of God, you feel compassion for the hurting, and you feel joy for those that are thriving. You are able to live in a doom and gloom world with love for each other. God connects you in spite of all the differences.

"And over all these virtues put on love, which binds them all together in perfect unity."
– Colossians 3:14

Hard-Core Beads

I picked up the Indian bead even though it wasn't exactly what I was hoping for. This one had a hard center. I like the Indian beads with holes through the middle. If I wanted to string them, I didn't have extra work drilling a hole. Not every Indian bead comes like that though.

When we think about it, not all of our blessings come the way we want them to. We easily recognize blessings when they fall unexpectedly into our laps—when we haven't done much to get them. But just like the hard-core Indian bead that takes more work to put a hole in the middle, some blessings take more effort. They are still blessings even when they don't easily fall into our lap.

Your job, your relationships, your situations may take more work on your part, but they are still blessings from God. Not all blessings come easy.

Be thankful for the hard-core blessings.

"That each of them may ... find satisfaction in their toil—this is the gift of God."
— Ecclesiastes 3:13

Conquering Old Baldy

Weko Beach has a few dunes but nothing like "Old Baldy." Old Baldy is a huge dune at Warren Dunes State Park located along the shores of Lake Michigan. When I was a kid, my family would go there. Some days, we would climb Old Baldy before heading home. From the bottom, it always looked so big and formidable to me. I kept my eyes down as I climbed one step at a time until I reached the top.

Sometimes we face things in life that seem too big to handle. Situations may seem impossible. They can discourage us right from the start. We see what we face and it's too much.

There is a way to handle those impossible situations. It's living by faith ... keeping your eyes on the path God leads you in and doing what you can do one small step at a time, believing in His Word as you go. Before you know it, God has helped you to the top. Climb the big, impossible dunes one small step at a time and focus on Him.

"If you have faith as small as a mustard seed ... nothing will be impossible for you." – Matthew 17:20

Go Get It

Most summer days there are people walking Weko Beach with their dogs. Some dogs lie around near their owners. Others walk alongside them. What I enjoy most is seeing the owners throw a stick or a toy out into the water. The dogs eagerly jump in to fetch it.

We are into Jesus. We go to church every week. We read our Bible every day. Our thoughts are directed by Him.

Does it bother you when you don't see others maintaining a healthy relationship with Jesus? They may not know of Him, but here in the USA, that's probably not true. What keeps them from Him? Maybe the hypocrisy of a Christian or the judgement someone feels. If you and I would throw out what others want, then maybe they would jump in and go after Jesus.

Give others a reason to WANT to go into the water.

"We are therefore Christ's ambassadors, as though God were making His appeal through us." – 2 Corinthians 5:20

Stolen Bread

I watched the sea gulls chaotically gather around the couple as they tossed breadcrumbs into the air. The couple tossed a bread crumb meant obviously for a specific sea gull but another bird swooped in and stole it. The sea gull wasn't ready.

I don't doubt at all that there is enough of God to go around. So why doesn't everyone have Him in their life?

The Bible tells a parable of a farmer sowing seed and some of it grows while some of it does not. Why? Because of the environment the seed lands in. When God's Word is tossed like breadcrumbs to its intended recipients, the environment—your heart, your soul, and your mind—has to be prepared for it. I have learned that it is my responsibility to always remain open and favorably disposed to the Word of God so it doesn't get stolen away like a sea gull stealing bread crumbs.

Don't let the precious BreadCrumbs get stolen from you.

"As he was scattering the seed, some fell along the path, and the birds came and ate it up."
- Mark 4:4

Pressing Clouds

Michigan has days when the sun doesn't come out. It gets lost behind the clouds. Cold snow, the frozen lake, and a dark day, even on a beach, can change one's mood from bad to worse.

What do most of us do when we have bad days? We focus on what's wrong. We lose sight and hope for what's beyond the problems. It's like going to the beach on a winter day focusing on the cold snow, the frozen lake, and the dark day. We wonder if the sun will ever shine again.

When you walk with God, you have a small idea of what He is capable of. You know His love for you. You have hope. Life will still press in on every side, but you know the sun will shine again. God, in His love, has not forgotten you and will not abandon you.

With God, the sun still shines in spite of the pressing clouds.

"We are hard pressed on every side, but not crushed; perplexed, but not in despair; persecuted, but not abandoned; struck down, but not destroyed." – 2 Corinthians 4:8-9

Looking through the Windshield

I got out of my car and noticed someone sitting in the car next to me. I'm not sure what brought them there, but I have done the same thing. I sit in my car facing Lake Michigan on a tough day, needing the escape of the beach while not wanting to be around others.

All of us have tough days—days where we need an escape … some place we can run and hide … a place to calm us down.

Even though the beach is my go-to place when I need a break from life, there are times I feel so defeated and broken all I can do is sit in my car. It is enough in my brokenness to see the waves behind the windows while locking everything else out. God calms, heals, and gives hope when nothing else can. It is enough to look for Him in the middle of it all.

When life gets tough, look through your windshield for God.

"My flesh and my heart may fail, but God is the strength of my heart and my portion forever."
– Psalm 73:26

Two-Fold Footprints

I studied the footprints as I walked along the beach. By the size, you can usually tell if it was a man or a woman. You can tell if it is an adult or child. As I studied, I left behind my own footprints.

The way people live their lives says something about them. It tells us where they are in life in their relationship with God. It's like footprints giving us clues to who is walking along the beach.

But there is the other side too—your footprints. The way you live your life says something about what is important to you and where God fits in your life. It can tell others what you trust in or what you hope for.

Footprints serve two purposes: to lead you to or away from others and to consider what you stand for and leave behind.

"By their fruit you will recognize them. Do people pick grapes from thorn bushes, or figs from thistles?" – Matthew 7:16

Trash Talks

I wondered if I should continue writing this book. I had a lot of ideas but I wasn't sure I would have enough for 365 days. That's what was going through my mind as I walked along the beach until I came across my answer.

When we need answers or direction, where do we go?

I used to think the only way I could know what God was leading me to was to hear it in a sermon or to read it in the Bible. He felt distant as I struggled to understand what He expected of me. But God doesn't lock Himself up behind the walls of a church or only pen His ideas on the pages of the Bible, so why would He limit Himself to those things when revealing what He expects of us? He can show us what He wants anyway He chooses.

I found direction that day starting with a pen tossed away on the beach.

God can talk through trash.

"For the sake of Your name lead and guide me."
— Psalm 31:3

Cold Water

It was sunny and warm. Lake Michigan should feel warmer than it was. I stepped back out of the cold water.

Doesn't God seem cold and distant at times? Bad things happen, and we wonder where He is. Our prayers don't get answered. We don't hear from Him so we move forward on our own without Him. He seems as cold as Lake Michigan.

When I felt the cold water, I pulled away from it. I distanced myself from the coldness. But that's not how to handle it when God seems cold. King David felt that same way and what did he do? He chose to trust God even when God felt far away. He chose to sing praises to God, remembering His faithfulness and unfailing love.

Put your feet back into the cold Water.

"How long, Lord? Will you forget me forever? ...
I trust in Your unfailing love ... I will sing the
Lord's praise, for He has been good to me."
- Psalms 13:1-6

The Nails Shine Through

The nails kept the boardwalk in place. I didn't have to worry about stepping on a board and it slipping out from underneath me. It was there, secure as could be.

Jesus had the most important calling God ever gave to anyone. He died on the cross to take away our sins so we could spend eternity in heaven. He is the Son of God yet He came down as one of us and allowed all of our sins to crucify Him on the cross. He could have done anything to stop it. He had the power. But He didn't. He allowed us to nail Him on the cross.

The more you go through life, the more opportunity there is to realize your need for the nails in Jesus hands. The times you feel unloved, the nails shine through. He could have loved Himself more than you and taken Himself off. The times you feel hopeless, the nails shine through. He was not defeated. He overcame and He is there for you to overcome too. The times your mistakes overwhelm you, the nails shine through. He prayed on the cross for those mistakes. "Father, forgive them, for they do not know what they are doing." Your mistakes were forgiven. Shiny nails secured our place in eternity.

"They crucified Him there." - Luke 23:33

Get Out of the Car

Some days I arrive at Weko Beach ready to go. I pull up, park the car, and step out. I look over the row of cars near me and usually notice a car or two with people sitting inside. I think to myself, *"They aren't getting the most out of the beach sitting there in their car."*

Comfort zones affect decisions. If it falls inside our comfort zone, we don't hesitate. We probably aren't even thinking about comfort. If something is outside of our comfort zone, there is more of a chance we won't step out and do whatever it is. We experience it in church when we don't volunteer because of fear or inconvenience. The problem is … we can't experience all God has for us unless we step out. It's like going to the beach and never getting out of your car. You don't feel the sand in your feet or the coolness of the water.

Get out of your car and experience all the Beach has to offer.

"The blessing of the Lord brings wealth, without painful toil for it." - Proverb 10:22

In the Dark

Weko Beach stays open until 11:00 pm each day. I finish my walks before it gets dark, but when I was younger that wasn't always the case. Occasionally I would walk with others along Lake Michigan in the dark.

Don't we feel lost when change comes? We are thrown out of the familiar into something new. We are in the dark, not knowing what's coming next or how to handle things.

Jesus offers you what the world cannot and will not. When change comes and you are feeling lost, Jesus is the answer. He is the light shining in your darkness. He has the answers you are looking for and, even if He chooses not to show you those answers, He is the hope you need. You don't have to grope in the dark alone. Jesus may not take the changes away, but He will shine His light on things so you do not remain in the dark.

Walk with the Light on a dark night.

"I am the light of the world. Whoever follows Me will never walk in darkness but will have the light of life." - John 8:12

Hope for an Indian Bead

Lake Michigan washes up the Indian beads I collect, and it can wash them away.

Broken dreams. Failed goals. They leave us hurt and lost. They make us feel inferior from our lack of accomplishments.

God can give you dreams and take them away just like Lake Michigan can wash away an Indian bead. You can place your hope in them, but they are temporary. The impermanence of life has taught me where to put my hope. Not in my dreams that only last until they are accomplished or broken, but in an eternal God. Hope in God never fails because He is eternal. He is faithful. So, when God allows your dreams to slip through your hands … when He allows dreams to be accomplished leaving you unsure of what's next, hope in Him. He will carry you through.

What do you put your hope in … a dream or God?

"But God will never forget the needy; the hope of the afflicted will never perish." - Psalm 9:18

Hot Air

The balloon lay lifeless on the sand. At one time it was full of air carrying it from its origin to its final destination. Now the air was gone, and the balloon was no longer able to rise above the sand.

We base our lives on our abilities, our money, our circumstances, and on other people. At some point they fail us.

Building your foundation on anything other than God can leave you deflated. The substance of anything else will eventually give out and cannot help you rise above life's circumstances. But God is not full of hot air. He is the foundation that carries you throughout your life. He doesn't leave you stranded like a deflated balloon unable to rise above the sands of life.

Evaluate your foundation. Choose the one not full of hot air.

"For no man can lay any foundation other than the one already laid, which is Jesus Christ."
- 1 Corinthians 3:11

Retreat to the Water

I couldn't get into the water fast enough. The walk down to the water's edge was almost unbearable. The flies were biting like crazy.

"When it rains, it pours." Life has its ups and downs. We love the up times but could do without the down times. One bad thing after another happens just like tiny little flies biting, one right after the other.

You have a place to go when problems won't let up and when one bad thing happens after another. That day, I hurried into the water hoping to find refuge from the biting flies. God may allow problems into your life, but He also gives you a place to retreat to.

When the flies keep biting, retreat to the Water.

"You are my hiding place; You will protect me from trouble and surround me with songs of deliverance." - Psalm 32:7

Letting Go

I used to have a beautiful golden retriever named Sam. He was a hyper-friendly dog so when I took him to the beach for a walk I was afraid to let him off the leash.

Some of the hardest moments in a parent's life involve letting go of our kids. It starts at a young age when they go to gatherings without supervision. We are no longer there to guide their social choices. Then there's the day they are able to drive alone. Along comes college and they move into the dorms or a college apartment. Life has a lot of letting go moments for parents and it can be scary. We don't want to let them off the leash like I didn't want to let Sam off his.

I finally realized that my children would miss out on so many good things if I didn't let them go. I want them to experience the blessings I experienced as an adult, and I don't want to take that away from them. I had to learn (and I'm still learning) to trust God where my kids are concerned.

Let them go and trust God with them.

"When I am afraid, I put my trust in You."
- Psalm 56:3

Seasons Change

I have experienced all four seasons on Lake Michigan: the newness of spring, the height of summer days, the falling leaves of autumn, and the frozenness of winter. Each brings with it its own ups and downs.

Our lives change. We experience changes in the seasons just as on Weko Beach. Experiencing change goes way beyond seasons. Our bodies change. Our attitudes change. Our circumstances change. These changes can make life difficult to navigate.

The Bible says Jesus never changes. When you wake up one day struggling with things you have done a million times, Jesus hasn't changed. When you are developing new attitudes, He hasn't changed. When the steady and reliable circumstances of your life change, He hasn't.

Jesus is the constant in your changing world.

"Jesus Christ is the same yesterday and today and forever." - Hebrews 13:8

Grains of Sand

If sand is dry it is easily brushed off, but if it's wet it's not so easy. The worst is when it gets in your hair. You can shower it out thinking you have gotten it all until you feel the grains of sand later on.

Some situations in life are not easy to get over. They hang onto us like wet sand. We do what we can to wash it off and, maybe most of it is washed away, but every once in awhile the situation rears its ugly head again like finding grains of sand from another time still stuck to our head.

Whatever the situation, God's got you covered. Whether you are at fault or not, He is there, willing to wash you clean 100%. He is there for those situations you easily get over, and He is there for the hard ones that linger beneath the surface—ones you may desperately try to hide. God is there for you. He sees the issues you may not even know are still buried inside, and He loves you anyway.

Water washes away the hidden grains of sand left from life's struggles.

"Wash away all my iniquity and cleanse me from my sin." – Psalm 51:2

Live Picture

I looked over the horizon and could see Lake Michigan moving with each wave. I could see the details all around. In the distance I could see where the lake met the sky. The live picture stopped there.

When we go through hard times, it's easy to lose sight. We see the situation and that's all we see. It's like looking out over Lake Michigan and not being able to see past it.

I have been in circumstances I thought would never change. I could have felt defeated (and there were days I did feel that way) not knowing the changes in store. The nice thing is that, although life is constantly changing, God doesn't change. Tough situations don't last forever. Your pain heals and new hope comes. Focus on the One who doesn't change. He is a good God and promises to bring good from your tough situations. When you feel defeated by your circumstances, the goodness of God is the hope you and I find in every circumstance.

The picture doesn't stop there.

"I the Lord do not change. So you … are not destroyed." – Malachi 3:6

Endless Water

I looked out over Lake Michigan. It was as if the smooth water went on forever. It was so peaceful and calm.

There are things in life we depend on: our families, our friends, our jobs, our abilities. We naturally expect them to be there every day, but things change.

It can be scary when everyone and everything you depend on falls short. It can knock you down. When family disappoints you, when friends desert you, when companies let you go, when you can no longer do what you use to do, what are you left with?

I looked out over Lake Michigan and was reminded of an everlasting God—One who doesn't change. You can depend on Him. He is always there when others aren't. He is there when you feel like you can't even depend on yourself.

Dependable endless Water.

"The Lord is the everlasting God. ... He will not grow tired or weary, and His understanding no one can fathom." – Isaiah 40:28

Beach Day

When my kids were young, I planned out their week. I scheduled time for reading and time for writing. We had craft days, friend days, and, of course, a beach day. On beach days we packed up our toys, the sunblock, and plenty of food.

The things important to us are the things we make time for. I wanted my kids to enjoy Lake Michigan so each week I set aside an afternoon for Weko Beach.

When God is important, when you want to bring Him into your life, you make time for Him. You make time to go to church once a week. You make time to read His Word every day. He is on your mind all the time. It's like setting a beach day. You schedule it and you follow through because it is important to you.

Go ahead and schedule a regular beach day with God.

"Keep this Book of the Law always on your lips; meditate on it day and night, so that you may be careful to do everything written in it."
– Joshua 1:8

Enjoy While You Can

I got out of my car to head out on my walk. An older gentleman was sitting in the car next to mine with his window open. "Enjoy it while you can," he said with a smile.

Don't we sometimes take God for granted? We go about our days as if there is always another day to spend time with Him. It's like assuming it's always summer on the beach.

God is a patient God. He loves you enough to let His Son die to have a relationship with you. Don't take Him for granted. There came a time in the Old Testament when the Israelites didn't hear from God for a long time. One of the purposes for my walk that day was to enjoy the sun while I could. Approach your relationship with God the same.

Enjoy Him while you can!

"Seek the Lord while He may be found; call on Him while He is near." - Isaiah 55:6

Transparent Stones

In the middle of all the stones on the beach was a small white stone. It was different than the others and almost looked transparent.

We can feel uncomfortable when we are different from others. We don't want to be different. We hide what we are really like in an effort to not attract any attention to ourselves.

Have you ever felt that way? I have. I don't like being different and I don't like others seeing right through me with all my faults. But that's exactly the way it should be. When you accept Jesus into your life, you are different. Your life changes and becomes more transparent. The differences and the transparency of your life may be what draws others to Him.

Embrace your transparency.

"So that you may become blameless and pure, 'children of God without fault in a warped and crooked generation.' Then you will shine among them like stars in the sky." - Philippians 2:15

Pictures from the Past

When we were done eating our ice cream bars, we walked around inside the Beach Town Grill. Looking at the old pictures displayed from the past, it was interesting to see the beach had not changed much.

The faithfulness of God is evident from generation to generation. The old Weko Beach pictures displayed His faithfulness. The beach was not only still around, much had not changed. God's faithfulness allows our world to continue, blessed with the environments and societies we live in. His faithfulness expresses the love He shows us through the simple blessings … like a peaceful day along Lake Michigan … like good memories shown in simple old photographs.

Pictures from the past are a reminder of God's faithfulness today.

"Because to the Lord's great love we are not consumed, for His compassions never fail. They are new every morning; great is Your faithfulness." - Lamentations 3:22-23

Forms of Water

Water can be seen all around Weko Beach. There is the lake and the stream. There are bottles of water and a drinking fountain. There is a shower to wash off sand and, on rainy days, there is rain.

In our struggles to see God, we may miss Him because we have a certain view of Him in our minds. In reality, God works and shows Himself in many ways like water at Weko Beach showing up as a lake, a stream, a bottle of water.

When you struggle in your search for God, maybe it's time to rethink things. Instead of trying to see God through your preconceived notions, take a look at the things around you. Consider how God is revealing Himself through them, whether it is in the waves of a lake, the ripple of a stream, or the flow of a drinking fountain. It's like going to Weko Beach and seeing more than just the lake.

Water shows itself in different forms.

"He is the rock, His works are perfect, and all His ways are just. A faithful God who does no wrong, upright and just is He."
- Deuteronomy 32:4

Lifeguard Needed

Some beaches have a lifeguard on duty. Weko Beach is not one of them. Still, safety is important. Instead, Weko Beach offers warning signs about the dangers of riptides and places life rings strategically along the lake.

Lifeguards are all about safety. They watch out for potential problems, avoid distractions that take their eyes and mind off why they are at the beach, and they are always ready to rescue anyone physically in harm's way.

Life offers many potential things to trip us up. It's normal to be on guard for your own physical safety. No one wants to get hurt. But what about your spiritual safety? The Bible talks about guarding your heart. What does that mean? What you watch, what you read, the places you go, the people you hang around with, the thoughts you dwell on, the priorities you set—all affect the condition of your heart which affects your spiritual well-being.

Lifeguard needed … to guard the heart.

"Above all else, guard your heart, for everything you do flows from it." - Proverb 4:23

SPF

When I was a teenager, going to Weko Beach was all about getting a nice tan. Sun tan oil with little or no protection from the sun's rays was my favorite. I wasn't concerned about SPF levels.

Don't we have our minds focused on the here and now? Bills, to-do lists, today's circumstances—it's all about today and how to deal with the things we face right here and now, much like a teenager focusing on getting a tan now and not worrying about the health effects down the road.

God's Word tells you to set your mind on heavenly things. That is, focus on the long term instead of the short term. How do you do that? Make long-term decisions—decisions based on the eternal outcome.

Choose the lotion with a high SPF.

"Set your minds on things above, not on earthly things." – Colossians 3:2

Flowing or Stagnant

There were little pieces of nature floating by telling me the water was moving. In some places, the stream rippled quickly towards the lake. In other places, it was stagnant.

How's your relationship with God? How's your faith? Every now and then, take a step back and evaluate. It's like walking along the stream at Weko Beach and considering: Is the water moving or is it stagnant?

When your relationship with God is moving—when it is active—it is alive and well. When nothing is happening, it is stagnant like a stream that's run its course. The Bible talks of people who believe Jesus is the Son of God and that He rose from the dead and conquered sin, death, and hell. When you believe, you have the Spirit living ... flowing inside you. Your faith—your relationship with Jesus—is not dead.

Is the Spirit flowing or stagnant?

"Whoever believes in Me, as the Scripture has said, rivers of living water will flow from within them." – John 7:38

Season Pass

I laid the money down along with my registration. In return they gave me a season pass—a sticker allowing me to get into Weko Beach for the rest of the summer. I stuck it on the lower left-hand side of my windshield.

It's easy to think we are not worthy or acceptable in today's world. We have to pay to fit in, to be accepted, much like paying for a pass to get into Weko Beach.

You can't change how the world operates, but you can be sure you are accepted by God. There is no longer a price to be paid for His acceptance. You see, Jesus paid the price in full. You have an eternal pass to God. All you have to do is accept it.

Stick your eternal pass up in your windshield. You've been accepted.

"He was delivered over to death for our sins and was raised to life for our justification."
– Romans 4:25

Trustworthy Sign

I was surprised to see the wooden sign showing where Weko Beach ended and Warren Dunes State Park began. It was quite a way down the beach. Obviously, the water had carried the sign to its new resting spot. It now marked in error where the beaches began and ended.

We trust the signs we read. Road signs direct our way. The labels on medicine guide our use of them. We make decisions based on the things we read.

There is nothing more trustworthy than the Word of God. It can direct our way through the unfamiliar circumstances of life. It can warn us about the perils of too much of one thing and not enough of another. It is truth, and truth can be trusted.

God's Word does not change and cannot be moved like a drifted sign along Lake Michigan. It will not mislead you.

"Blessed are those who keep His statutes and seek Him with all their heart—they do no wrong but follow His ways." – Psalms 119:2-3

November

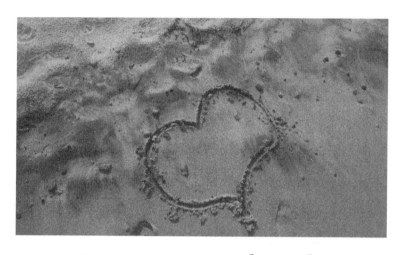

"Leave a message in the sand."

A Beautiful Sunset

Around nine o'clock or so, the sun sets over Weko Beach. People start gathering. Some set up chairs or blankets along the water. Others sit on benches on the boardwalk. All are there for one purpose—to see the beautiful sunset.

Don't we all want a good life? A good life is one well lived. Many people think God is just here to help with our life after death, but He is here to help with life now. He offers good advice to guide us clear of wrong choices that threaten to take the good from our life. He offers advice to guide us into better choices with the potential to make life even better. And there is comfort and strength for those with their eyes set on Him during the hard times.

Set your eyes on God throughout your life and be glad. When your time comes, you will leave behind good memories for those sitting there watching your beautiful sunset.

"I keep my eyes always on the Lord. Therefore my heart is glad." - Psalms 16:8-9

Empty-Handed Days

I walked and walked, but nothing. It was not a good day for Indian beads. I would be going home empty-handed.

There are times when we walk through life feeling empty-handed. Those are the days when nothing seems to go our way, when we are just getting by. They're the days when things aren't looking up and nothing seems to work out the way we hoped. We can't see the silver lining. It's a lot like taking a walk on the beach and not finding any Indian beads. The beads are there, but we don't see them. Our blessings are there, but we don't always see them either.

Those are days of opportunities to exercise and increase your faith. When you go through empty-handed days, you can choose to put your faith in God, to believe He can and will turn things around. You can choose to believe He is silently working behind the scenes for your good.

Empty-handed days become days of opportunities for faith.

"Now faith is confidence in what we hope for and assurance about what we do not see."
— Hebrews 11:1

Written in Sand

I walked along noting each letter as I went. I'm sure I have done the same thing—written in the sand leaving a message behind for future beachgoers.

Did you know the way to show your love for God is through obedience? God wants us to love Him so much that He writes what is important to Him on our hearts and in our minds. He does that so we know how to love Him. Jesus lived a life of obedience to God which showed His love for God and left behind the words "I love You.".

With each day comes a new opportunity to write a new message. What's your message going to say? Will it show a love for God? Will it show love for others? You are the author.

Leave a message in the sand.

"I will put my laws in their hearts, and I will write them on their minds." – Hebrews 10:16

The Veteran

Near the Beach Town Grill entrance is a large rock. On it are chiseled words explaining when and why Taps is played as the sun sets. It's a special moment when the music starts. People stop. They pause at what they are doing out of respect to all who put their lives on the line for our freedom.

We have a book. It tells of a Saviour who paid the price. He fought the war and gave His life. He died to set us free from the hold of sin and eternally from the consequences of our sin—death. The book tells of the sacrifice He made. May our songs cause us to stop—to pause out of respect for what He has done—for the freedom we have. Greater love has no one than this: to lay down one's life for one's friends. Jesus laid down His life to save us from our sins and from eternal death.

Let's pause out of respect for what He has done.

"Through Christ Jesus the law of the Spirit who gives life has set you free from the law of sin and death." – Romans 8:2

Beachgoer's Love

When the kids were younger I worried about them swimming. I'm not a good swimmer. I wondered if I'd be able to help. On those days I wished Weko Beach had a lifeguard.

Life is too hard to go it alone. There will be times when we need others and times when they need us.

Even though there wasn't a lifeguard on duty on at Weko Beach, there were other beachgoers who probably would step out and help. Your spiritual walk can (and should) have others around ready to step in and help, to keep you safe and to point you in the right direction when you are out of your element. They look out for you spiritually as you would for them. After all, that's a beachgoer's love in action.

"Love your neighbor as yourself."
— Mark 12:31

Let the Rock Speak

On the rock near the entrance to the Beach Town Grill are the words, "God is nigh." I thought how true that is.

We can't always sense God's presence. We fall into the trap of thinking He can only be found in church, and His words can only be found in the Bible. We sometimes fail to realize His presence anywhere else.

God is nigh whether you sense Him or not. He is with you in all you do, whether at church or on the beach or somewhere else. It's heartening to know you have Him right beside you as you live out your life. In difficult times when you feel totally alone, God is there. You are not alone. He can talk with you wherever you are. In the good times, He is there to share your joy.

Let the rock speak. God is nigh.

"The Lord is near to all who call on Him, to all who call on Him in truth." – Psalm 145:18

Peaceful Sleep

I stretched out on the beach blanket. The sun felt warm on my back. The waves brought a steady peaceful sound, putting me to sleep.

Mentally crossing off things from today's to-do lists, thinking ahead about tomorrow and what is going on, running a tough situation over and over again in our minds—it can be hard to turn our minds off at the end of the day and get a good night's sleep.

You know what put me to sleep on the beach? The warm sun and the peaceful sound of the lake. It's easy to wind down when you have hope, when the future is warm on your back. It's easy to wind down when what (or Who) you rely on is dependable. It brings peace. When you listen to God, you have hope. You have so much peace that falling asleep is not a problem.

The sound of the Water brings peaceful sleep.

"In peace I will lie down and sleep, for You alone, Lord, make me dwell in safety." – Psalm 4:8

People Watching

One day as I was people-watching, I saw a mom yell irately at her children, a family packing things up together, a couple not walking together, and teenagers tossing a Frisbee back and forth.

People behave in different ways in different situations, and we watch what they do.

You can learn from people whether they are doing the right thing or the wrong thing. You can learn what is right in a situation and how to go about it by watching others. You can also learn what and how to avoid situations by watching others going through it and handling it wrong.

Blaming the environment you grew up in (or one you are in right now) only goes so far. People make mistakes. People do wrong things. Each of us can learn from a "good" person and from a "bad" person, from a good environment and from a bad environment. What you learn and choose to do with the people watching is what really matters.

"Let the wise listen and add to their learning, and let the discerning get guidance." – Proverb 1:5

When the Beach is Not In

The sun was hidden behind the clouds and few people were at Weko Beach. Summer was over. Going to the beach was out of season and no longer the "in" thing.

Some of us have to be in on the "in" thing. It's important to us. It's easier to be "in" than on the "outs."

There may be seasons in your life when God is "in" and others seasons when He is not. It's at those times you are faced with a decision, an opportunity, to decide how important He is to you. You decide where and when He fits into your life. The Bible tells us to put Him first. One of the ways that is done is by choosing Him all the time, even when following Him is no longer "in."

Choose the Beach even when it is not "in."

"But seek first His kingdom and His righteousness, and all these things will be given to you as well." – Matthew 6:33

Dow7nward Boardwalk

I climbed the boardwalk. It was all fine and dandy heading up, but now it was bringing me back down.

Don't we all have days where our best efforts and intentions lie broken on the ground. The goals we set, that we believe we were called to do, are still unmet and we've messed up. Why do we continue to mess up on what we were called to do?

Boardwalks may lead you downhill. It's not always an upward climb and it's not always a level path. When things seem to be headed in a downward direction, it's easy to think you've gotten off track. But God uses both the up times and the down times. Jesus, although the Son of God, had a life full of ups and downs, from miracles to the crucifixion. Don't think you messed up your calling because circumstances don't seem successful. God is in control and may have intended things to be just this way.

Boardwalks were made for walking up and walking down.

"But God intended it for good."
— Genesis 50:20

Favorite Bathing Suit

When I was a little girl, my mom bought me a beautiful bathing suit. I loved it. Every time we went to the beach, I was excited to wear it. It had big, bright turquoise, purple, and pink flowers on it. One day, I lost the bottoms.

We place so much value on temporary things. Maybe it's our homes, our cars, our bank books, our looks, our status.

God warns us about what we treasure. He gave some good advice though: Build up treasure in things that can't be stolen, that won't rot, and that can't be lost. I got over the disappointment of losing my favorite bathing suit years ago and, you know what? I still treasure things about the beach. But it's not a bathing suit. It's my time with God, learning from Him and finding peace in Him. Those are the things God was talking about. The lessons He teaches can't be taken away. The peace He gives stays with you even when all is lost, including your favorite bathing suit.

"Do not store up for yourselves treasures on earth, where moths and vermin destroy, and where thieves break in and steal."
– Matthew 6:19

Fences in the Way

Snow fences hampered the way to the water's edge. They were planted all over the beach blocking a clear path to the lake.

Obstacles. We find them in our paths and we place them in the paths of others. They can cause us to quit trying and make life difficult as we strive towards our goals, much like the snow fences on Weko Beach.

We can't control the obstacles others place in our paths, but we can keep trying, and we can control the obstacles we unconsciously lay in the paths of others. The Bible ties our judgement of others to obstacles we place in their way. When we judge others, we set up fences blocking their way to God.

Take down the fences. Stop judging.

"Therefore let us stop passing judgement on one another. Instead, make up your mind not to put any stumbling block or obstacle in the way of a brother or sister." - Romans 14:13

Turn to the Water

I stepped on something and cut my foot. It was a little disappointing as a kid to be sitting on my towel trying to stop the bleeding when I could be swimming.

Some of us find ourselves sitting on a beach towel disappointed and angry. We turn away from God.

You may have unresolved feelings because God allowed situations that hurt you. I have been there. They brought me to the lowest point, but I learned something. I could turn from Him or I could turn towards Him. It was turning towards God that helped me stick around long enough to see the healing He brought after the heartaches. Just as water heals our wounds, God heals our hurts.

Get off your beach towel and turn to the Water.

"Then they cried to the Lord in their trouble, and He saved them from their distress. He sent out His word and healed them."
– Psalms 107:19-20

Searching Eyes

It has become a habit. My eyes search the sand along my path look for another Indian bead. I can't help but hunt for them when I'm there.

How's life going? Are you finding your blessings or have you given up? Are you looking for them, like hunting for an Indian bead on Lake Michigan?

God does the same thing. His eyes roam the earth. He looks to and fro, ready to hand out blessings to the blameless. If life hasn't gone your way … if you've given up expecting anything good … keep looking. Keep expecting. His blessings may not be what you are looking for, but they fit into His perfect plan for you. His blessings are better than anything you could come up with. So hang in there. Look for the good your eyes may have overlooked.

Don't give up. Keep on looking. God's blessings are out there.

"For the eyes of the Lord range throughout the earth to strengthen those whose hearts are fully committed to Him." - 2 Chronicles 16:9

Packing Up

As a young kid, it was never fun to pack up at the end of a day on the beach. My mom made each of us carry something to the car and, if someone was not carrying something, she heard plenty about it.

Teaching lessons from God's Word seems illusive to a parent. It's hard to see our efforts in the day-to-day routine of life. We come to the end of some days wondering if we really taught our kids anything.

My mom probably didn't realize at the time that she was teaching me Scripture when she made each of us kids carry stuff back to the car. I didn't even realize it as a child, but now, years later, I see the lesson. I learned not to just think of myself, but to pitch in and help.

God's lessons come in everyday happenings. We may not always see it, but as parents living out His Way, we naturally teach it to our children.

Packing up—a lesson along the way.

"Not looking to your own interests but each of you to the interests of others."
– Philippians 2:4

At the Bottom

We found ourselves sitting on a sled at the bottom of a sand dune at Grand Mere. With cold snow in our faces we sat there looking up at the dune we just came down.

We face our mountains in life. They can be big—a struggle to overcome—and they keep us wondering and worrying about the outcome.

God knows your struggles. He sees you struggle at the height of your problems, and He knows you worry about them. He provides help like a sled cutting a path down a snowy winter dune. Put your hope and trust in Him. He provides a way.

Some day you will be sitting at the bottom of your cold mountain looking up with snow in your face and realizing where your help comes from.

"I lift up my eyes to the mountains—where does my help come from? My help comes from the Lord, the Maker of heaven and earth."
– Psalms 121:1-2

Smile

The word "SMILE" was etched out in the sand. I didn't feel like I had much to smile about, but it got me thinking …

To be honest, I never really liked it when people said "smile." I found it a little annoying, but it was that simple word written in the sand that changed my attitude and my focus that day. By the end of my walk, I felt much better about the circumstances that brought me down to the beach, and I thought about the things I can be thankful for—things to smile about.

Too many times we focus on our problems. We let them steal our joy and our smiles. Maybe the little things we point out to each other and the little things we say to each other make a difference. They can encourage us and point us on towards a better day. Think about what you say to someone. Think about what you do. Think about how you encourage them.

Leave a "smile" in the sand for someone.

"Therefore encourage one another and build each other up."—1 Thessalonians 5:11

Pick a Spot

When we arrived at the beach, I didn't care where we set up camp. If it were up to me, I would have picked the first available spot we came across. But that never happened. We walked along the crowded beach looking for enough space to fit a big family. The spot had to be near the water, and it had to have direct access without other beachgoers in the way.

As a parent I pray for my children to find their spot in life. I pray it will be near to God. I pray others won't get in their way and stand between them and Him.

There never seemed to be any rhyme or reason to the spot we wound up at on the beach. Sometimes life seems like that – no rhyme or reason. But walk on until you find your spot. God has a way of leading you to where He wants you. Trust Him. He will do the same for your kids.

Pick a spot near the Water.

"In their hearts humans plan their course, but the Lord establishes their steps." – Proverb 16:9

911 Box

Near the Beach Town Grill is a 911 box. I've never seen anyone use it, but it's there for emergencies.

We deal with emergencies differently. We may all know to call 911 first in case of an emergency, but when put to the test, not all of us do that.

When trouble happens, who or what do you run to first? God tells you in His Word to call Him when there's trouble and He will help you. Before trying to fix things on your own, before running to your significant others, before worrying, before giving up, turn to God in prayer. Acknowledge His love and care for you. Acknowledge His ability to handle the situation and then entrust it to Him.

Go ahead. Make the call.

"Call on Me in the day of trouble; I will deliver you, and you will honor Me." – Psalm 50:15

Water and Imaginations

Crossing oceans to foreign lands on an air mattress, fighting off sharks lurking beneath the water, spinning around as if getting flushed down a toilet—water and imaginations. Fun in the water can be found in simple things.

Some of us grow up and lose the ability to have fun—to enjoy life. It's like sitting on the beach and not knowing what to do. Nothing comes to mind.

I love thinking back on those imaginary experiences created on Weko Beach. I can still hear the laughter. I can still feel the joy as we encountered each turn of our imagination. God blesses you and I with life. We're not here just to grow up and take care of responsibilities. He gave us the ability to imagine, to laugh, and to enjoy. Even today, the joy those memories give still comes alive.

Let go and enjoy the life God has given you.

"He will yet fill your mouth with laughter and your lips with shouts of joy." – Job 8:21

Shades

The sun was bright. I put on my shades. (Are they even called that anymore?) It dimmed the brightness.

There have been times in my life that I wanted to know every little detail and plan God had in store for me. I wanted to "help" Him get me there. In hindsight I'm glad I didn't know some of those details. I'm glad I didn't see it clearly coming. I would have been defeated before I even began.

It's a blessing and a benefit to not know everything God has planned for you. Your defining moments may come through the struggles He has planned. If you know what's coming, you may try to avoid it and miss it. Trust in God is built when you rely on Him. When things aren't so bright as the sun on a summer day and you can't see as clearly with your shades on, an opportunity rises to trust in the God who does see. He knows how much you can really handle in each moment.

Shades can be a blessing from God.

"Now I know in part; then I shall know fully,
even as I am fully known."
– 1 Corinthians 13:12

Time to Go

"Time to go." That's the last thing a kid wants to hear at the beach. I didn't like hearing those words. It meant my time was done when I was just getting started. I wanted to stay. I wanted to enjoy it more, but it was … time to go.

We love to be in God's presence. We love hearing His Words and singing His praises. We love church. We love the peace and the freedom we experience near Him. We don't want to leave it. We don't want to face a world without peace or freedom. But God calls us … time to go.

You can't accomplish what God has instructed you to do, to go out into the world representing the Good News to others, when you stay in your "Christian" environment. The ones needing to hear the Word most likely are not near God or that environment you love so much. He calls you to go.

It's time to leave the Water and give the Good News.

"Go into all the world and preach the gospel to all creation." – Mark 16:15

Painted Foot

Years ago my friend and I found this stone on the beach. In our youthful, vivid imagination it looked like the top half of a foot—toes and all. We took it home and painted it. It's still here somewhere, decorated in paint from long ago.

Some of us are really good at things. We are like a stone decorated with talent. It's easy to get a big head because of our abilities and accomplishments. It's hard to remember where we get them from when we are the ones putting in the practice and work to improve our skills.

Your abilities come from God. He gives you the natural talent, the time to practice, the drive, and the financial resources. He determines how talented and successful you will be.

God is the one who decorates your stone.

"It is God who judges: He brings one down, He exalts another." – Psalm 75:7

Twinkling Light

The airplane lights twinkled in the darkness over Lake Michigan. They looked like tiny stars hanging low in the sky pointing out the direction to the Chicago airports.

Our choices tell who we are and what we support. People watch us. Those choices can point them in the right direction or they can point them in the wrong one.

When you make choices to do the right thing … when you make choices in line with God's Word, you are like an airplane flying through a dark night with lights pointing others in the right direction. The Bible tells you to let your light shine. The choices you make and the way you live are the lights people need to see in a dark world. It glorifies God.

Be a twinkling light.

"In the same way, let your light shine before others, that they may see your good deeds and glorify your Father in heaven." – Matthew 5:16

Surprise Story

I am always surprised by some of the things I find washed up along Weko Beach. I wonder what the story behind it is. I wonder what events led up to it being in the lake and how it ended up on the beach.

As adults, nothing should surprise us. Expect the unexpected. Isn't that usually the norm these days? It's like taking a walk on Weko Beach only to come across something so out of place. It makes you wonder.

God is full of surprises. One story after another of unexpected surprises can be found in the Bible. From creating everything out of nothing … to an old (I mean real old) husband and wife having a child … to raising people from the dead … God is full of surprises.

What's your surprise story?

"I will surely return to you about this time next year, and Sarah your wife will have a son."
– Genesis 18:10

Frozen Beach Glass

The ice on the lake had broken up into many, many small, clear pieces that could have easily been mistaken for pieces of beach glass.

When things work out our way … when we get something unexpected … when good news comes and everything shines like a summer day … when we stumble upon tons of "beach glass" along Lake Michigan … we are blessed.

So much of life can be spent trying to find and hang on to our blessings. But maybe we've got this wrong. Maybe the small pieces of beach glass don't compare to the abundance of frozen ice pieces. Maybe God can't be compared to the blessings He gives us throughout life. He is more valuable than all of them. He lasts when many of the blessings we chase after end. He is perfect at all times. He doesn't become dated and useless as time goes by.

The blessing of God in your life is way more abundant than any other blessings you get along the way.

"And God is able to bless you abundantly."
– 2 Corinthians 9:8

Beach Chairs

I walked around the beach chairs. You know, those low-to-the-ground chairs made especially for the beach. They were sitting in the shallow water. Growing up I rarely placed my chair in the water. I always sat farther back.

Life is full of many opportunities and choices. It can be hard deciding among them. Some things appeal to us more than others.

You make a choice every day on how close you will be to God. The things you do, the thoughts you think—all are choices bringing you closer to Him or pulling you farther from Him. It's like deciding where you set your chair on the beach. Will you set it farther away and watch from a distance or will you set it in the water?

Set your chair in the Water and soak in It.

"You will fill me with joy in Your presence, with eternal pleasures at Your right hand."
— Psalm 16:11

Seeing Red

I sat in my car looking over the dark sky above Lake Michigan. Night was well on its way. The sky towards the southwest was almost red, reminding me the sun was still out there somewhere.

Hope. It's what is needed in difficult times. It's what gets us through. It says it will not always be this way. It is the red sunset seen from a distance in the surrounding dark of night.

I can't think of a better Bible verse giving hope than John 3:16. We have a God who loves us so much He gave up His Son for us. No matter how difficult life gets, this tells us we are loved and there is hope. Even if the situation never gets better, we know heaven is in our future; it will get better. We have a God who loves us and a Son who spilt His blood for us. We are promised we will never walk alone. That is our hope in this dark world.

Are you seeing red in your dark surroundings?

"For God so loved the world that He gave His one and only Son, that whoever believes in Him shall not perish but have eternal life." – John 3: 16

Single Set of Prints

Many times I walk Weko Beach alone. I look at the footprints before me and see them walking together, but I leave behind my single set of footprints.

There are times in life when we go it alone. We may not want it that way, but it happens. Things seem to stick out more in those alone times … like the single set of footprints in the sand.

Although I left my lonely footprints on the beach, many times I was not alone. My footprints would have shown one person, but they didn't show Who walked beside me. God carries us along life's paths though others may not see. He becomes our companion in lonely times. He provides us strength to go it alone. Time with Him establishes a close and intimate bond that no one else can see … like an extra set of footprints walking next to the lonely ones you leave behind.

"He gathers the lambs in His arms and carries them close to His heart." – Isaiah 40:11

The Beachgoer

Even in the mainstream, I can always tell a beachgoer from everyone else. Maybe it's the bathing suit straps showing under their clothes or the smell of suntan lotion as they walk by. Maybe it's the beach bag they carry.

Following God means we are different—something most of us try hard not to be. We don't want to stick out from the crowd.

It's a good thing to be different. It's a good thing to stick out, especially when it's because of God. The way you live, the way you think, the things you say … God changes it all and makes you different. That's one of the ways He is represented and others learn about Him.

Be a beachgoer that is different from the crowd. Put God on. Carry His Word in your heart.

"Do not conform to the pattern of this world but be transformed by the renewing of your mind."
— Romans 12:2

December

"Life is better with the Water."

All In

The first thing I do is put my feet in the lake. There is a purpose for that: to find out the temperature of the water before deciding to swim or not. If it's too cold I don't go in.

What are the things stopping us from going all in with God? Is it a little discomfort? Or maybe it takes more of a commitment then we are willing to make? We may make a decision whether or not to swim based on the temperature of the water, but do we make our decision to follow God, to chase after Him based on our comfort level?

To be a follower of God, you have to be all in. You have to deny yourself—your comfort, wants and goals. It shouldn't matter if the water is too cold or not. To be all in for God means you are going to follow Him regardless of your comfort level.

Cold or hot—all in.

"Whoever wants to be My disciple must deny themselves and take up their cross daily and follow Me." - Luke 9:23

Small Beads

Another small bead. I picked it up and headed home. Don't get me wrong. I was glad to have another Indian bead to add to my collection, but I like the big ones the best. I went home feeling a little disappointed.

Bigger is better. That's how the world sees things. Maybe that's why I walked away feeling disappointed.

Jesus' way of seeing things is different. He saw a woman giving a small tithe while others were giving big tithes. He didn't see the size of the tithe and leave it at that. What He saw was what each person did with their gift. The poor woman gave a bigger tithe from the small resources she had.

You don't have to be disappointed with your small blessings. It's how you use them that make the difference in God's eyes, not the size.

Small blessings can have a big impact.

"But she, out of her poverty, put in everything— all she had to live on." - Mark 12:44

Wet Sand Castles

Have you ever noticed that building a sand castle takes wet sand? As a child trying to build the perfect sand castle, I quickly learned to go to the edge of the water and fill my bucket with wet sand. Sand castles aren't built with dry sand.

Don't we get caught up and mistakenly try to build our own lives by ourselves? We think we can handle it. We overestimate ourselves. We may even subconsciously believe we don't need God. Then the fragile, dry life we built comes sliding down.

Truth is you need God to go through life. Just as I learned that wet sand works better than dry sand to build my castle, life works better with God than without. You can't do it on your own so turn to Jesus to receive the Holy Spirit's help.

Life is better with the Water.

"Repent and be baptized, every one of you, in the name of Jesus Christ for the forgiveness of your sins. And you will receive the gift of the Holy Spirit." - Acts 2:38

Beach Worship

I walked past the group on the beach. It was obvious it was a church gathering. I could hear their words and I saw them bow their heads in prayer.

Most of us are comfortable with worshipping God in church. But it's wonderful to be able to worship Him anywhere … including Weko Beach. Let's not let location limit our worship. Worship at home, in the grocery store, on the beach … God is worthy. Our worship should be so Spirit-filled it cannot be contained by buildings or kept behind closed doors. It cannot be held quietly inside. It should permeate our lives—lives lived out daily in worship by our attitudes and desires, by a love so strong for God, our spirit wanting nothing but to praise Him for who He is and for all He has done, thankful for His strong hand and wisdom in our lives.

Worship God on the beach.

"Yet a time is coming and has now come when the true worshipers will worship the Father in the Spirit and in truth, for they are the kind of worshipers the Father seeks." - John 4:23

Lasting Footprints

Footprints in the sand are left behind by the beachgoer who went on before you. They remain for a while until the water comes and carries them away or the wind blows them away. They are gone without a trace.

For many of us, we want to leave a legacy behind. We work steadfastly throughout life to do just that. We want to believe what we do will ultimately have a lasting impression.

Do you want your life to have a lasting impression? The Bible says heaven and earth will pass away, but God's Word will remain. Everything else you do in life will not last unless it involves the Word of God. It's like the footprints left behind in the sand. They vanish without a trace. Living by the Word—deciding what to do in light of it—makes your efforts last.

Will your footprints leave a lasting impression?

"Heaven and earth will pass away, but My words will never pass away." - Luke 21:33

Foggy Days

The fog rolled in. It covered the lake as the cold water met the unseasonable warm air. The beach looked different.

What do we do when change happens? People handle things differently. Some of us face it head on. Some go with the flow and adjust. Others ignore it, hoping it will go away.

Change sometimes requires looking at things differently. It may require a change of heart. God may allow changes in your life you didn't really want but know that He has everything you need to handle it. He can give you a new perspective on things, enabling you to move forward. It's like seeing the beach differently. not on a sunny hot day, but on a foggy, unseasonably warm day.

A change of heart comes when looking from a new perspective.

"I will give you a new heart and put a new spirit in you; I will remove from you your heart of stone and give you a heart of flesh." - Ezekiel 36:26

Sunday Mornings

Songs could be heard as people filled the Beach Town Grill. It was a Sunday morning church service at the beach.

One of my favorite things on Sunday mornings is being around like-minded people, singing and worshipping God. I imagine it's a small taste of what heaven will be like. Problems and struggles are set aside for a sacred time of worship. They feel small in comparison to God's love.

Early Christians devoted themselves to learning, fellowshipping, communing, and praying. They made a point to learn God's Word. They made a point to get together with others of the same mind-set.

There are many options for church offering different styles of learning and worshipping. Pick one and devote yourself to it.

Sunday morning church on a beach. How does that grab you?

"They devoted themselves to the apostles' teaching and to fellowship, to the breaking of bread and to prayer." - Acts 2:42

But I'm Not on the Boardwalk

Not everyone walks the boardwalk.

It's easy to see a pastor's or a Christian singer's calling. The words of God flow out of their mouths. It's harder to see the calling of a janitor, a cashier, a garbage person, an office clerk …

You may be that janitor, cashier, garbage person, or office clerk. You love God and you want to be a part of His plan. You may look at your life and wonder what your calling is. It's a lot like looking at others on the boardwalk who know where they should be. You are on the outside thinking, "But I'm not on the boardwalk."

God has a calling for you, and it may not be on the boardwalk. It may be walking along Lake Michigan or sitting on a towel in the sand instead. It is still a calling. Every calling involves serving others with the talents and gifts God has given you.

Not everyone is called to walk the boardwalk.

"Each of you should use whatever gift you have received to serve others, as faithful stewards of God's grace in its various forms." - 1 Peter 4:10

Colors of Sand

My son collects sand from different beaches. The sand comes in a variety of colors—white, red, black, tan.

Probably all of us at some time have compared our lives to others. The comparison can lift us up or bring us down. Our lives are as different as the colors of the sand.

Have you ever been disappointed with your life? Have you wondered why things are the way they are? Sure, disappointments happen and life may not seem as good as the lives of people around you. But God allows every experience in your life to glorify Him. When I look back at the disappointments in my life, God trusted me with the awesome responsibility to handle each one of them. My sense of responsibility grew, and each disappointment became an honor to represent Him in the middle of it.

Be glad whatever color sand you end up on. Do the best with it and let God be glorified. It's an honor.

"But this happened so that the works of God might be displayed in him." – John 9:3

Golden Reflections

I looked out over the evening waters. The sun was going down, shining its golden reflection on the surface.

It's easy to make a spur of the moment decision without considering its effects. In hindsight, it could be good or bad. It's like walking Lake Michigan and looking for the sun's reflection—a good, shiny, gold reflection or a not-so-good, poor reflection.

How do you make decisions? Do you consider how it will affect you and others down the road? Will you be okay with it at the end of it all, looking back in hindsight? When you consider your decisions in the light of God's Word, you can't help but see a shiny, golden reflection. God steers you into ways you won't regret, ways you can be proud of.

Take time to evaluate your decisions in light of God's Word, then …

Look for your golden reflections.

"I have considered my ways and have turned my steps to your statutes." – Psalm 119:59

Into the Lake

If you walk along Weko Beach, you will see a stream running from the campground out to Lake Michigan. The stream flows steadily into the Lake.

Don't we sometimes get it messed up? We think life is all about us. We get upset when things don't go our way. It's like expecting the lake to flow into the stream. When it doesn't, we don't understand it.

It's easy to understand that life is not all about you. When situations happen and you are put out, that's when it gets hard. It's hard to understand why you get the small end of the stick when someone else clearly is at fault. It goes against human nature to put up with it. You don't need a reason to humbly take what you don't deserve. Jesus took the punishments for the wrongs you did. Maybe it's time you did the same ... for the glory of God.

Streams flow into the Lake, not the other way around.

"For from Him and through Him and for Him are all things. To Him be the glory forever! Amen."
– Romans 11:36

Crackling Ice

The strange sound took me off guard. Not something I remember ever hearing at Weko Beach before. Many small pieces of broken ice floating on top of the lake were bumping into each other creating a crackling sound.

It can be hard on tough days to feel close to God. Our hearts aren't in it.

On days when things aren't going right, when you see your wrongs and how far you fall short in your walk with God and the hardness sets in, you may find it difficult to praise Him. In those times, stop and listen. What do you hear? You may hear the birds chirping or the wind blowing through the leaves on the trees. You may hear dogs playfully barking or the laughter of people. All are praises to God—praises that may turn things around for you causing you to sing yourself.

Can you hear the crackling ice?

"All the earth bows down to You; they sing praise to You, they sing the praises of Your name."
– Psalm 66:4

As Needed's

I sat in the car looking out over Weko Beach. I was nearing the end of writing this devotional and running out of ideas. I worried that I would never come up with enough to finish it.

Truth be told I prefer to have everything lined up before I even start something. Isn't that typical for many of us? We want to know all the details. We want to know how we will get from point A to point B.

The Israelites complained to God about the lack of food and He sent them manna. He instructed them to gather only a day's worth. They had to trust God to provide more the next day.

God provides only as needed as a way to test you and to build your trust in Him. He did for the Israelites and He did for me.

Trust God for your "as needed's."

"The people are to go out each day and gather enough for that day. In this way I will test them and see whether they will follow My instructions." – Exodus 16:4

Touched by the Water

In an empty parking spot lay broken glass. I moved along, looking for a place to park my car.

Some of the things we run after end up not being worth the effort. They bring harm instead of good. It's like thinking broken glass is beach glass. It can cut you. It can cause pain.

Have you ever had a time where everything worked out just right? Nothing was planned. You made no effort and there it was. It all fell into place without your planning or your effort. When God blesses you, you know it. No pain comes along with it. The difference between the blessings we strive for and the ones meant for us is the touch of the Master's hand.

Don't mistake broken glass for beach glass. Beach glass has been touched by the Water.

"The blessing of the Lord brings wealth, without painful toil for it." - Proverb 10:22

A Comfortable Walk

When I go to Weko Beach, I head down to the water on soft sand. But as I get closer to the water, I can feel the stones on the bottom of my feet. It's not soft like the sand. It doesn't feel good and is a little uncomfortable. At times it can actually hurt.

Following Jesus is not easy. The closer we follow Him, the less comfort we find. It's like walking closer to the water. We leave the soft sand and walk on the hard, stony pebbles. It can be uncomfortable and may even hurt at times.

When you follow Jesus, you aren't promised an easy life without problems. In fact, the Bible says the opposite. You will be misunderstood, made fun of, persecuted. As a Christian following Jesus, you ignore the temporary discomforts and …

Find your comfort in Him along the stony path.

"Everyone who wants to live a godly life in Christ Jesus will be persecuted." - 2 Timothy 3:12

Stay on Track

I had this great idea to take the kids to the beach. When I got there, I loaded up the stroller and set off to find a place. The problem was that once I hit the sand, the stroller didn't work. I struggled to drag it to the nearest spot.

Raising kids is a very important task that's not easy. We, as parents, may feel we are up against the world when it comes to teaching them and putting them on the good path. It's a struggle much like dragging a stroller through the sand.

Please be encouraged today. You are not alone. Many parents before you faced the same struggles—to grow responsible, loving, and caring adults out of our young children. When your efforts are just wheels spinning without traction, when you are dragging them more than they are walking alongside you, just keep going. Familiarity has a way of bringing your aging kids back to their roots.

Stay on track.

"Start children off on the way they should go, and even when they are old they will not turn from it." - Proverb 22:6

A Good Walk

A young couple strolled by walking ankle deep in the water. Many couples walk along Weko Beach. Some talk as they walk while others quietly stroll together enjoying the moment.

Why do couples take walks along the lake? It's positive. It enriches their relationship. They spend time together in a peaceful environment away from the distractions, and they reconnect.

God is good. He is good for your relationships. Just as a walk along the beach enriches your life and the lives of those sharing your walk, God enriches you. He is the break from the distractions. He is the peace in your environment. As you reconnect with Him, He helps you to reconnect with others.

Couples go to the beach to enrich their relationships. We all can go to the Lord. He is good for us.

Take a good long walk.

"Give thanks to the Lord, for He is good."
— Psalm 107:1

The Chase

It was an unusual winter on Lake Michigan. Usually the water freezes over, but not this year. It was mid-February. The lake didn't freeze, but ice formed on the cement water sanitation structure.

When we are wronged, our hearts can become calloused and hard. Sometimes we intentionally choose to let that happen as a way to protect ourselves. We become like water on top of the sanitation structure in the middle of winter—frozen and cold. We are nothing like the unfrozen water still in the lake.

It's not easy to forgive time and time again. It's easier to shut ourselves off, but that comes at a price. It may not be easy but chasing after God's heart keeps our hearts in good condition. It's choosing to handle the situation as He would handle it and as He directs you to handle it, letting God protect your heart and trusting Him to heal the hurts you have. A person after God's own heart chases after His heart.

What are you chasing?

"I have found … a man after My own heart; he will do everything I want him to do." – Acts 13:22

Run to the Water

The young children squealed and ran to the water. I remember those days well, arriving at Lake Michigan with such excitement. My siblings and I would drop everything and run straight for the water. Our excitement and enthusiasm could not be contained.

Our love for Jesus can grow old. We may take Him for granted. Our excitement and enthusiasm doesn't come out as it did when we first committed to Him.

Take time every once in a while to evaluate where your relationship with Jesus stands. How's your attitude toward Him? Are you restrained in your excitement for Him? Are there responsibilities keeping you from spending time with Him? Can you rearrange your schedule to make time with Him first? If the excitement is gone, are you living in faith, giving Him room to do the unimaginable?

Get excited again. Run to the Water.

"You were running a good race. Who cut in on you to keep you from obeying the truth?"
– Galatians 5:7

Splattered Sand

I wasn't too happy when my kids playfully kicked sand and water all over me as we walked towards the car. The wet sand ended up on the back of my legs after I just washed off minutes earlier.

Every one of us has been hurt by the actions of others whether intentional or not. We do what we can to make our lives what we want them to be and someone does something to hurt us. We find wet sand splattered all over our clean lives.

You don't have to be ashamed of the hurts others have caused you. You don't have to be discouraged or hide because of it. We have all been there. God is right there all the time, ready to help. That day on the beach when my kids splattered wet sand on me, I was walking along the water. I went to the water and easily washed it off. When people hurt you, go to God. He walks alongside you, able to wash away the hurt you feel.

You don't have to be afraid of splattered sand. It washes off with the Water.

"The Lord is with me; I will not be afraid. What can mere mortals do to me?" – Psalm 118:6

Strength of a Stone

The stones on the beach are hard, durable, able to withstand the powerful waves. There were no shortages of waves today.

Most days it's easy to go about a normal day. We have the knowledge and the ability to handle a regular day. It's like seeing yourself and what you can do as a hard, durable stone, able to withstand every powerful wave coming your way.

Have you ever found yourself in situations you never expected—situations beyond your control? You reach a point where all you know how to do and all you are able to do isn't enough. You simply can't do anything more to change the situation. It's in those moments you realize that you can't trust in yourself. Your own knowledge and abilities aren't enough to pull you out of the situation you find yourself in. You've met a wave too powerful to handle.

God is strong enough for every powerful wave.

"It is better to take refuge in the Lord than to trust in humans." – Psalm 118:8

Fishing from Shore

Three fishing poles were set up along the beach. Their lines reached out into the water. It surprised me. I don't know much about fishing, but there didn't seem to be much chance of catch anything from there. Chances seemed better going out on to the lake. I asked the man about it. He reassured me salmon could occasionally be caught from the shore.

When we try to win people over for God, we have it in our minds how things ought to work. We think we know the best chances for winning them over. The problem is, our plans never seem to work the way we think they should.

God knows what He is doing. He knows where the catch is and how to go about catching it. He told the disciples to throw their nets on the other side of the boat. It made a difference when logically it shouldn't have. If God tells you to fish from the shore, listen. With Him, anything can happen.

"Throw your net on the right side of the boat. ...
When they did, they were unable to haul the net
in because of the large number of fish."
- John 21:6

Turn the Lights On

We sat there in the car. We could hear the water but it was too dark to see it. As we got ready to leave, we turned on the headlights. It was only then that we could see Lake Michigan's white caps. The light from our car highlighted them in the dark from a distance.

Sometimes we make a half-hearted attempt in our effort to find God. We know what we should do and we do it, but we don't take time to go that extra mile. It's like going to the lake at night to see the water. We sit in the car with the headlights off unable to see what we came for.

It wasn't until we turned on our headlights that we actually saw the lake. Take time. Make the effort to connect and find God with all your heart.

Don't just sit in the car. Turn the lights on to find the Water.

"You will seek Me and find Me when you seek Me with all your heart." - Jeremiah 29:13

Beyond the Dingy

Two young men were swimming out past the dingy. This was not unusual. At Weko Beach there are usually a few people who go beyond the safety of the dingy.

Probably most of us don't want to venture out beyond our safety zones … beyond the dingy. We like to be where it is safe and comfortable. We understand things in our own little enclosed world and we like it that way.

Life with God is not always safe and comfortable. He calls you to go beyond yourself, your abilities, and your comfort zones so you can rely on Him more. God chooses you to go past the familiar and live beyond what you can do by letting Him do what He can do through you. It's basically an opportunity to build faith.

God may call you to swim beyond the dingy.

"You did not choose Me, but I chose you, and
appointed you so that you might go …"
— John 15:16

Frozen Over

In the winter when the water freezes over, it's hard to tell where the sand ends and the water begins. It's almost as if there is no water.

I have had days when I felt the need for God and I couldn't find Him. All of us have probably had days like that. We want God. We need Him but it seems like He is nowhere to be found. As I grow, I look back on some of those times and God was there. I just couldn't see Him or what He was doing at the time. It's a lot like Weko Beach frozen over in the winter. All you see is the ice. You don't see the water underneath. It's easy to see your problems and feel the coldness they bring to your life, but God is there. Satan makes your problems stand out so you focus on them.

God hides Himself to increase your faith as you focus on Him.

"Now faith is confidence in that we hope for and assurance about what we do not see."
– Hebrews 11:1

Brought to Attention

Here I was on Weko Beach feeling disappointed and down. It didn't help to see others around me laughing and enjoying time with each other. Their togetherness caught my attention and brought me down.

Not everyone values the same things. It shows in the way we live our lives and how we spend our time.

You've chosen to follow God. You've chosen to put your trust, faith, and hope in Him. You've chosen to live life His way. Now you find yourself around others who may not feel the same way you do. You feel like a lonely beachgoer alone on a beach full of other beachgoers. It hurts. It's disappointing and can get you down.

Others may not value God as you do, but your desire for Him is right. While you may not be able to control what others choose, you can bring them to God in prayer.

Go to the Water and bring them to His attention.

"My heart's desire and prayer to God … is that they may be saved." – Romans 10:1

Exercise Your Appreciation

It was my first day in the exercise class. I listened as they talked about what they enjoyed most about the class—the people, the view, the environment. They held the same appreciation I have for Weko Beach.

There's something to be said about who we hang out with. It says something about who we are and what we like. It's nice to be around people who feel the same way we do and who have the same interests.

The Bible recognizes the differences between people. It recognizes the uncommon ground between those who love God and those who don't or those who are indifferent to Him. When we surround ourselves with people who love the same things we love, we are building an environment around us that encourages our growth in that area. That's why it's important to surround yourself with others who love God just as you do.

Join a class to exercise your appreciation for what's important to you.

"What fellowship can light have with darkness?"
– 2 Corinthians 6:14

Darkness

I've been to the beach on nights when it was so dark you couldn't see much of anything. Even the water was hard to see. I would almost believe it wasn't there if I couldn't hear it.

It can be difficult to see our way in hard times. We see and feel our problems. They are dark and gloomy. They drown out everything else just like a dark night on the beach. We can't see the answers we desperately need. We may not even sense God's presence.

One of the things I have learned is that God may purposely hide Himself in those times. It goes against what we expect of Him. We expect God to be there, to be our hero, to make everything right, to light up our dark days. When God hides Himself, He creates an opportunity for us to trust and exercise faith in Him. Faith is active and real when we live in the dark and wait for Him to provide the light.

Have faith in the middle of the darkness. God is there.

"He made darkness His covering, His canopy around Him—the dark rain clouds of the sky."
— Psalm 18:11

Your Choice

I choose to go walk the beach regularly. It's important to me. Something I look forward to each week. So when my family doesn't go, I feel it.

Not everyone makes the same choices, and those differences are reflected in many different areas of life including the choice to believe God. As Christians we may especially feel it when those close to us don't actively pursue a relationship with Him. It gets us down. We feel like we are the only one on board for a day at the beach.

I don't have the answers. Even Jesus' brothers didn't believe He was the Son of God. Jesus knows what it is like to have close family and friends who don't believe. He can relate. The one thing I do know is that your relationship with Jesus is important. It is worth pursuing with or without family and friends. It is the one relationship you cannot do without. After all, your pursuit of Jesus says something, and that may be the very thing that gets others thinking.

Choose the Beach anyway.

"For even His own brothers did not believe in Him." – John 7:5

Frozen Mind

It was hard to enjoy my walk. I couldn't concentrate or think about much else. Even bundled up in my winter coat, I was still cold. I struggled as my mind kept going back to how frozen I felt.

The winter seasons of our lives can be a struggle. Those are the days of problems—days where all we see is what is wrong—days with no solutions in sight. Our minds feel frozen, focused on our problems, unable to get past them.

When you face tough winter days, it's hard to stay focused. Those are the days to purposely choose to read your Bible and stay in the Word. Those are the days to memorize a few Bible verses and apply them to the situation. It can be a struggle just as it is walking along Weko Beach in the cold, winter weather.

Thaw your frozen mind with the Word.

"Set your mind on things above, not on earthly things." – Colossians 3:2

My Walk on Weko Beach

It started with an Indian bead on a bad day. An inaudible lesson touching my life, speaking to me about what hurt most down deep inside me. I listened, and I came back week after week for more to heal my wounds and to encourage me on.

I learned that God is good. He cares about each of us and what we go through. He can teach us through His Word, but also through His creation. Through those seemingly small, insignificant thoughts we have as we walk through life God speaks to us, guiding us through difficult decisions, rejoicing with us in good times, providing hope as we look forward to the next step, teaching us lessons from simple, everyday things, and growing us beyond what we are capable of.

I learned that it wasn't my walk on the beach I needed; it was my walk with God.

Walk with Him.

"Speak to the earth, and it will teach you ... that the hand of the Lord has done this."
— Job 12:8-9

Made in the USA
Columbia, SC
19 December 2023

28842967R00211